Historical and Social Dimensions
in African Christian Theology

Historical and Social Dimensions in African Christian Theology
A Contemporary Approach

Wilson Muoha Maina

WIPF & STOCK · Eugene, Oregon

HISTORICAL AND SOCIAL DIMENSIONS IN AFRICAN CHRISTIAN THEOLOGY
A Contemporary Approach

Copyright © 2009 Wilson Muoha Maina. All rights reserved. Except for brief quotations in critical publications or reviews, no part of this book may be reproduced in any manner without prior written permission from the publisher. Write: Permissions, Wipf and Stock, 199 W. 8th Ave., Suite 3, Eugene, OR 97401.

Wipf and Stock Publishers
199 West 8th Avenue, Suite 3
Eugene, Oregon 97401

www.wipfandstock.com

ISBN 13: 978-1-60608-124-2

Manufactured in the U.S.A.

For my parents,
Wangari na Maina wa Ngunju
Ngemi ciumaga na muciĩ
Wega umaga na mucii

Contents

Acknowledgments / ix

Preface / xi

1. The Area of African Theology Is an African Social and Historical Context / 1
2. The Social Nature of the Christian Faith and the African Historical Context / 24
3. Method in African Theology / 52
4. The Christological Foundation in African Inculturation Christian Theology / 84

Bibliography / 115

Acknowledgments

I AM GRATEFUL TO the editorial staff of Wipf and Stock, who tirelessly worked preparing the manuscript for publication. Jim Tedrick, Diane Farley, Christian Amondson, and others were all very helpful from the initial stages to the final publication of this work. Amanda Price copyedited the work, and her suggestions greatly helped improve the final manuscript.

I acknowledge the support of my colleagues in the department of philosophy and religious studies at the University of West Florida: Sally Ferguson, Nicholas Power, Lawrence Howe, William Mountcastle, and Joulanda Garber, the office administrator. Special thanks to all the students I have met in the classroom. They have been a tremendous inspiration in the development of some ideas in this work.

Preface

IF ONE WERE TO ask whether there is a need for an African Christian theology, the answer would be found in the reality of African Christianity.[1] The very presence of vibrant churches in Africa calls for thoughtful reflection, and this reflection is what African theology is about. For African Christians to have come to faith, they must have engaged themselves with what it means to be Christian in their lives and historical context. Hence, one can argue that the first theologians in Africa, or even elsewhere, are properly the people who make a profession of faith and live that profession every moment of their lives.

In a concrete way, Bishop Christopher Mwoleka of Tanzania clearly formulated the task of African theology. Presenting a paper at the Symposium of Episcopal Conference of Africa and Madagascar General Assembly in Rome in September 1975, Bishop Mwoleka pointed out important areas of doctrinal and pastoral research:

1. The manner of presenting and practicing Christianity. The radical but convenient way of making a transition:

    - from the religion of the commandments to the religion of the Good News;
    - from a servile religion to the religion of liberation from self-concern;
    - from the religion of self-centered individuals to the death of the ego and resurrection into the community;
    - from the Law of Moses to the Exultation in the Paschal Mystery.

---

1. By the year 2000, the estimated number of African Christians was 356,277,000: 114,316,000 are Roman Catholics, 87,190,000 are Protestants, 33,660,000 are Orthodox, and 20,551,000 are Anglicans [*World Almanac*]. See also Bokenkotter, *A Concise History of the Catholic Church*, 344. For more figures on African Christianity, visit http://www.adherents.com/adhloc/wh-2.html.

2. The theological expressions and terminology which will deliver us from the paralyzing demon of DUALISM.
3. The Spirituality of the Laity.

When these goals have been set, Christians mobilized, programmes conducted through and through, and continually revised; then, and only then, can we have some hope of ever advancing in the direction of restoring all things in Christ.[2]

What is the use of an African theology or any theology? It might sound like a simple utilitarian question; however, one does not engage the study of theology only for the sake of it. There has to be another purpose. Basically, in theology there is the unavoidable task of trying to understand our nature as human beings and our natural environment. From a theological and philosophical perspective, the assertion of belief in God fits into the human concern for an explanation of all of existence. Hence, the God-question is also a question about existence as a whole. Human beings are especially interested in the issue of meaning. The God-question fits, therefore, into the human concern for meaning and identity. Theology, then, is concerned with human beings asking questions about God, themselves, and the world. Further, the question of God has a social dimension. Generally, people live in community with other human beings. In an attempt to understand reality, one realizes that one is not alone in the universe but that, along with others, one is a participant in the quest for meaning.

The usefulness of theology is to be seen through the contribution it makes to humans living in society. Through critical analyses, theology brings forth understanding not only of faith in God but also an understanding of humanity. Theology is necessary in human living. To achieve its end, theology should have as its foundation the reality or issues that concern human life and their relation to belief in God. The foundation of theology lies, therefore, in the understanding of what it means to be a human person and the existential connection with God. There is a need to overcome the view that understands theology as abstract and as having no contribution to human living. Theology is studied in the context of the world, and for this reason, human experience in the world provides the basis for its study. The significance of African theology is in its foundation in the reality of human experience in Africa. If African theology does not

2. Mwoleka, "Small Christian Communities," 32–33.

Preface

reflect on African experiences, then it ceases to be relevant in an African context and is thereby a contradiction.

According to Paul Tillich, theology deals with the human questions about God. It tries to understand the human situation, which requires what Tillich calls courage. Courage implies hope in the search for understanding of the human person and the world. Tillich describes courage as an affirmation of one's being and further as an ethical act.[3] Theology is the study of God, and, "The question of God is the ultimate question of life; it is the single most important question facing men and women in the world today."[4] Dermot Lane is of the opinion that a theology that concerns itself only with the proofs for the existence of God is inadequate. This kind of theology "fails to point out the activity of God in the world and the restless searching of the human spirit. The problem with the proof approach is that it runs the risk of reducing God to the modal status of an object somewhat like a star or stone 'out there,' not unlike the rock of Gibraltar, which is incapable of affecting the individual on the personal level."[5] In the contemporary world, theology has moved from the concern of proofs for the existence of God to theology that emphasizes the historical involvement of God in human and world history. "The mystery of God is not some kind of theorem to be proved; it is rather, an experience to be lived."[6] The question of God belongs to today's human society.

In this work, I propose a historical and social way of analyzing Christian theology in Africa. An African Christology is viewed as the foundation to African Christian theology. I raise questions on some African theological developments that concern themselves with African historical past and pay little or no attention to the contemporary historical settings in the continent. Chapter one deals with elements of change in an African historical context. African Christian theology is presented as a response to changing circumstances in Africa. Further, chapter two analyzes the social nature of the Christian faith and makes a suggestion that the Christian religion has something to offer in an African social-historical context. Chapter three proposes methodological approaches in African theology. Inculturation as a theological method is presented as relevant in

3. Tillich, *The Courage to Be*, 2–3.
4. Lane, *The Experience of God*, V.
5. Ibid., vi.
6. Ibid.

Preface

African theology and the Small Christian Communities (SCCs) as a way of testing the relevance of theologies developing in Africa and elsewhere. Finally, the work explores in chapter four the Christological foundation in African inculturation Christian theology.

The theological method in this work is both analytical and comparative. The study is open to various theological approaches, such as biblical, liberation, political, and anthropological. However, the focus is generally the African historical context. The study opens by analyzing the changing African historical and cultural context and then progresses to critically evaluate various theological methods, such as inculturation and liberation, through the recent development of the so-called basic communities or the Small Christian Communities (SCCs). The SCCs are viewed as a hermeneutic basis for understanding and analyzing theological methods, such as political and liberation theologies and the anthropological method.

Biblical references in this work are drawn from the New American Bible (NAB) and the New Revised Standard Version (NRSV).

1

The Area of African Theology Is an African Social and Historical Context

AFRICAN THEOLOGY HAS THE task of showing the significance of the Christian gospel in an African historical and social context. However, African theology should not remain at that level of thought. It has to concern itself with the transformation of social situations of desperation to ones of hope and integral human well-being. One way African theology has responded to social issues is by appealing to methods of liberation and political theology. But one cannot avoid raising the question as to why African theologians are not coming up with a method that addresses social and political issues that are genuinely African other than appealing to foreign philosophical and theological systems of thought.

In this section, issues that shape an African theology are analyzed. The underlying issue is African history, through which all other issues are to be understood. Among the issues considered here are changed circumstances in different parts of Africa, which include religious diversity, transformation of the continent through modern education, conflicts due to civil wars and political instabilities, as well as poverty and related issues. All these issues mentioned here are considered as influencing or determining the task of an African theology. Toward the goal of an African Christian theology, the gospel in its entirety is viewed as offering a practical way of dealing with the issues affecting Africa today. Although African theologians refer to liberation theology as it is practiced in Latin America, the concept of liberation is viewed here as inherent in African history. Hence, some theologians and other writers or even leaders who have addressed issues of liberation in Africa are considered in this work. It is also important to analyze briefly the contribution of others outside the African context, and in this regard the contributions of Gustavo Gutiérrez in liberation theology as well as the political theology of Johann Metz are briefly evaluated later in this study. A suggestion is also made of the need to develop an African theological way of dealing with social issues.

Consequently, it is of great practical significance that the issues that concern Africa today be considered from an African approach. African theology has to have its foundation in concrete African setting. It should be a theology by the people and for the people of Africa. The strength of African theology, therefore, lies in accurate analyses of the African social and historical contexts today.

PART ONE

Issues Defining an African Historical Context and African Theology

Human living in contemporary Africa has been tremendously shaped by encounters with outside forces, such as the modern education, technology, industry, etc. Hence, in contemporary Africa, human life is no longer solely lived out in the fields—hunting, gathering fruits and edible roots, or looking after humped cows or camels. The majority of people are concerned with issues such as economic growth, free and fair markets, sustainable development, and other aspects of living found in any contemporary nation in the world. In so many places in contemporary Africa, people are concerned with careers and professional development. However, the incorporation of Africa into liberal capitalism and consumerism, as it has taken place in many African cities, is not a totally positive development, because it also leads to other ills found in any urban center such as homelessness, broken families, and chemical dependency, among others. As a result of the importation of foreign ways of life, many African people have experienced a cultural identity crisis. The preceding can explain the reason why many social-political and economic programs have failed, leading to a vicious circle where one problem is replaced by another problem, hence making the situation worse than it was before. For example, the International Monetary Fund's Structural Adjustment Programmes (SAPS) failed because they were an imposition from outside that paid little or no attention to the facts in an African socio-historical context.

It is reasonable to hold that a contemporary African context calls for a contemporary African theology. Christian faith has to address the changed cultural setting in Africa. It is to the changed times that theology should be conversing with. The relevance of Christian theology and faith should be seen by how well it is lived in a concrete African setting and how well it is a basis for religious, social, economic, and political transformation.

The continuous cultural changes in Africa call for a Christian theology that is always in flux yet faithful to the sources: the sacred Scriptures and the Christian traditions. The way human beings express themselves in cultural symbols, including language, points also to the necessity of cultural relevance and meaningful faith expressions. This is the task of African theology today. The issues that have shaped modern African history should be the raw materials for African theology. The introduction of modern education and with it new political, economic, and social-religious settings in Africa have brought about cultural and historical changes.

Below is an analysis of the changing African historical context. I consider the extent of change and issues inherent and contributing to the changing circumstances.

African History and Theological Analysis

When African history is mentioned, one cannot avoid thinking of colonialism and early missionary endeavors. Although there are many developments in African history, we cannot ignore the impact of colonialism and missionary work and all the other contacts Africa has had with the rest of the world. The African continent has been changing over time. Post-independence Africa has its share of problems as well as some developments, such as the recently ended civil war in Angola and unfortunately, the civil wars in the Democratic Republic of Congo and Sudan.

Evidently, Africa is responsible for the shaping of its destiny. History does not mean being stuck in the past. It is dynamic. It is the people who engage life every day and its events who thereby make history. In the same dynamism of history, African theology should not be held captive in the events of long ago but should engage history as it happens, flowing from the past to the present and the future. African Christian theology is the study of the reality of African events, and through analyses of events, it engages life as it happens, thereby keeping the Christian faith relevant.

African theology has an inescapable task of critically and analytically responding to historical events as they happen. Through critical analysis of human living as it unfolds in various political, social, and economic situations in different places in Africa, African theology would show its significance and provide practical solutions to concrete issues affecting people. The concern with events as they happen in African theology does not mean that the past is irrelevant. Through the study of the past, we understand the people's strengths and weaknesses. African theology uses the African historical context as its foundation. This can be said of any theological study. For example, James Cone has addressed, in his theology, the black experience of oppression and segregation in the United States of America. Cone cites his experience as a child in Bearden, Arkansas. He states:

> I remember Bearden because it is the place where I first discovered myself—as black and Christian. There, the meaning of black was defined primarily by the menacing presence of whites, which no African-American could escape. I grew up during the age of Jim Crow (1940s and early 1950s). I attended segregated schools, drank water from "colored" fountains, saw movies from balconies, and when absolutely necessary greeted white adults at the back of their homes. I also observed the contempt and brutality that white law meted out to the blacks who transgressed their racial mores or who dared to question their authority.[1]

Consequently, theology calls for a critical evaluation and analysis of history. Since theology studies God and people, the message of hope and fulfillment should always nourish the community in which it is done. The strong points of the past are upheld and the weaknesses done away with. As noted before, theology should not exclusively deal with the past and forget the present and the future. However, it is my view that African theology has concentrated on African traditional religions as they were in the past and not paid enough attention to contemporary African context. Unfortunately, some African theologians have laid a claim that Africans have no sense of future time.[2] Do cultures and customs not change over time?

African nations for the last forty years after independence have had to deal with issues of nation building as well as situations of political dictatorships, political mismanagement, and social and religious identity crises. What James Cone says of black theology in the United States of America can be said of contemporary Africa. Making an observation on

---

1. Cone, *Risks of Faith*, ix.
2. Mbiti, *African Religions and Philosophy*, 21.

The Area of African Theology Is an African Social and Historical Context

the history and development of black theology in the United States of America, Cone states:

> New times require new concepts and methods. To dream is not enough. We must come down from the mountaintop and experience the hurts and pain of the people in the valley. Our dreams need to be socially analyzed, for without scientific analysis they will vanish into the night. Furthermore, social analysis will test the nature of our commitment to the dreams we preach and sing about. This is one of the important principles we learned from Martin King and many black preachers who worked with him. Real substantial change in societal structures requires scientific analysis. King's commitment to social analysis not only characterized his involvement in the Civil Rights movement but also led him to take a radical stand against war in Vietnam. Through, scientific analysis, King saw the connection between the oppression of blacks in the U.S. and America's involvement in Vietnam. It is to his credit that he never allowed a pietistic faith in the other world to become a substitute for good judgment in this world. He not only preached sermons about the promised land but concretized his vision with a political attempt to actualize his hope.[3]

Just as the black experience in the United States has shaped Cone's theology, so also African history and experience provides a tool for theological study that is socially responsible. It is the best way to be grounded in theological study. While the sacred Scriptures and the church tradition are the basic sources of theology, theological study is tremendously shaped by the community of the theologian. African theology is a response to an African historical context. African history is usually broadly categorized as colonial and post-colonial. Some pertinent issues in colonial and post-colonial Africa are considered below.

African History as a Struggle for Liberation (or Independence)

The concept of liberation is not foreign to Africa. Independence movements in Africa fought for self-government and development. For example, Kenya's main goals of independence from Britain in 1963 were to fight for the right to own and use their land and freedom from external domination as well as to rid the society of ignorance, poverty, and disease (through the provision of health care). Independence is the opposite of dependence, but ironically, many African countries remain dependent

3. Cone, *Risks of Faith*, 47.

upon foreign aid and loans from the World Bank and International Monetary Fund.

The process of colonialism in Africa made many African people realize what they had lost through the coming of the Europeans to the continent. Before 1950s and 1960s, there was a longing in Africa for the days in the past when African people governed themselves without external interference. This was the concern of the independence movements, especially after the Second World War. Karigo wa Muchai, a Kenyan Mau Mau freedom fighter, narrated his experience during and after the Second World War as follows:

> In 1939 I went to live with my parents in Kiambu. The Second World War had just broken out and Africans were volunteering or being called to serve in the army. At first I had no desire to fight for the British . . . I spent four years in the army, moving from Ethiopia to Madagascar, Ceylon, India and finally Burma where I was made a corporal and placed in charge of a small transport unit . . . I remained in Burma from July 1944 until January 1946 when, with war over, I was returned to Kenya and discharged in June. While serving in the army we Africans were told over and over again that we were fighting for our country and for democracy, and that when the war was over we would be rewarded in trade and employment and could look forward to a much better life than the one we had left. For my part I was only hoping to be given a small piece of land somewhere and to be treated a little more decently by the Kenya Government [*colonial*] and white settlers . . . These hopes and dreams of mine were quickly crushed on my return home. The army talk was false propaganda intended only to get Africans like me to risk our lives for Britain and the white settlers of Kenya. The life I returned to was exactly the same as the one I left four years earlier: no land, no job, no representation and no dignity (brackets mine).[4]

Also enlightening on the situation in colonial Kenya is the story of Ngugi Kabiro as it was narrated to Donald Barnett. Ngugi Kabiro narrated his experience growing up in the Kiambu district in colonial Kenya in the 1940s and 1950s. His family land, in the Kenyan highlands, was forcefully taken over by British settlers. Kabiro had to go to Nairobi city,

---

4. Barnett, *Life Histories from the Revolution Kenya* (#1), 14. See also Olupona, "African Religions and Global Issues," 188, where he refers to colonial British land tenure system's adverse consequences for the Kikuyu people.

The Area of African Theology Is an African Social and Historical Context

where living conditions were deplorable. He lived in a single room with four other Kikuyu young men who also were displaced by the British colonial rulers. Kabiro cited oppression and violence by colonialists as having led to the formation of Kikuyu Central Association and later the Kenya African Union, ultimately the Mau Mau freedom fight for land and self-government (*uhuru*).[5]

In Kenya, the Mau Mau Movement fought for the Kikuyu right to use and own their land, and this came to include the whole country as it is known today. The Mau Mau uprising was a fight by peasants for land and freedom from the British colonizers. David M. Anderson states:

> Between 1948 and 1952, the displacement and 'repatriation' of Kikuyu squatter labour from the European farms, coupled with increasing land-hunger within Central province, provoked an influx of Kikuyu job-seekers into Nairobi area. Official estimates had suggested that there were some 30,000 African male workers in the city in 1948, 17,000 (or 56 per cent) of whom were Kikuyu. By 1952, the total African workforce had doubled to 60,000, but Kikuyu males now accounted for 45,000 (or 75 percent) of this total. By 1954, Nairobi was therefore dominated by displaced Kikuyu, including many women and children, the vast majority of whom were unemployed and living in gross poverty and overcrowded discomfort. It was thought that those who came into the city after 1952 did so merely 'to evade the uncomfortable and trying conditions' prevailing in the Central province as a consequence of the counter-insurgency campaign against Mau Mau.[6]

Systemic oppression ignited the movement for liberation and the need for independence, which in turn led several groups to combine forces to fight the colonizers. This unity was emphasized before and after the end of colonial rule. The Gikuyu, Embu, and Meru people of central Kenya could emphasize their similarity in language, culture, and unity of purpose to fight colonialism and establish self-government by Africans. They would say and sing: "*Ni boco yaguire thi tukienyurana, Gikuyu, Embu, Meru tuiguane*" (It was the bean that fell down when we were sharing it, Gikuyu, Embu, and Meru people let us be united). I can remember hear-

---

5. Barnett, *Life Histories from the Revolution* (#2), 10–75.
6. Anderson, "The Battle of Dandora Swamp," 159–60.

ing in Kenya the recording of freedom and nationalism songs expressing people's wish for freedom and land (*ithaka*).

Some people did not see any difference between the missionaries and the colonial powers. Both were seen as serving the same master—their home country. Jomo Kenyatta, the founding president of Kenya, would say, "*Gutiri ngurani ya muthungu na mubea*," directly translated, "There is no difference between the colonial master and the priest." However, not all missionaries came from the same country as the colonial administrators. For example, in Kenya's central province there were Italian Consolata Missionaries as well as Irish and English Holy Ghost Fathers. African independent churches came about because of Africans' disenchantment with the colonial and missionary churches. Independent churches interpreted and combined Christian gospel and African traditional religions.

The main concern in the struggle for independence in many African nations was the right of the Africans to own and use land. This struggle continues even after political independence and the establishment of self-government in many African nations. On land distribution after Kenyan independence, Mboya states:

> ... one of the most difficult of the issues facing some of the developing countries in this time of crisis: the land. Land use and land reform present us with manifold problems. In Kenya we had the problem of deciding whether foreigners should continue to have areas exclusively reserved for them and, indeed, whether foreigners should continue to hold land at all. Few will deny that the whole idea of reserving land on a racial basis, above all for foreigners, is totally unacceptable in an independent country.[7]

Unfortunately, the problem of land ownership still remains in some African nations. Land conflict and use of natural resources has been known to lead to ethnic clashes. Theological study has a responsibility to make a contribution in finding solutions to all conflicts between people.

However, after independence a certain African elite emerged to take power. Barnett writes of African petty bourgeoisie who were created by

---

7. Mboya, *The Challenge of Nationhood*, 12–13. See also Muga, "Just a Minute—Kenya's Colonial History Not Yet Told." Muga writes of, "... the indigenous leaders of the newly-independent country, who were only too well aware that whatever their credentials may have been as 'liberators,' their future careers in politics depended largely on the extent to which they were able to deliver on the promises they had made to their people, and especially land."

The Area of African Theology Is an African Social and Historical Context

the colonial powers to maintain their influence and presence after independence. Barnett refers to policy headlines such as, "A Disguise for the Recruitment of African Stooges and Frontmen" and also, "Nationalism: A Colonialist Substitute for Ideology."[8] He states, "The British master Plan is thus quite simple in outline: 'Carefully relinquish political control to a properly indoctrinated group of the "right kind" of Africans, i.e., those whose interests are similar to and compatible with our own, so that we retain economic control.'"[9] The Mau Mau and the peasants who fought for independence were thrown outside the margins of society, while the educated elite formed their own ruling class. Some of the African elites were collaborators with colonial rule (sons of colonial chiefs); others were overseas for studies, or in political exiles.[10]

From the above, it is evident that the concept and need for liberation is indigenous to the African continent. However, the Christian theological concept of liberation is distinctive in that it includes the understanding of true liberation as only possible through God's intervention in human history. Before African theology developed to recognize the need for liberation, the African people were fighting and dying for their dignity as human beings. For this reason, liberation in Africa should not be taken as a foreign concept, since the concept of independence is an African understanding of what it means to be human and can be coupled with religious teachings, such as in Christianity. Independence in Africa was also understood by the state of self-determination or freedom. Africans wanted their power of self-government returned to them from the colonizers. The African fight for political independence can be referred to as a struggle for human rights. Independence was meant to restore the dignity that was robbed of the Africans by colonization. Did this materialize, or is it still an illusion?

Abuses in Post-colonial Independent Africa

Post-colonial Africa has witnessed some of the worst abuses of human rights. From Idi Amin Dada in Uganda to Jean Bedel Bokasa in Central African Republic, Africans have been butchered and tortured. Many people in post-independence Africa have experienced hopelessness and

---

8. Barnett, *Life Histories from the Revolution* (#1), 6–7.
9. Ibid., 5.
10. See Odhiambo, "*Matunda ya Uhuru*, Fruits of Independence," 39.

ask themselves how they followed the wrong direction led by unsuitable leaders. To bring about any change in many African nations, it has unfortunately meant going back to their colonial masters to make or force their government to respect human rights; otherwise their former colonial masters would deny them the much-needed financial aid. This is a sad state—a state where people are made powerless over their own destiny. Democracy has not worked in many African countries where people's right to vote has been disenfranchised by vote rigging, not to mention intimidation through the use of state security forces. It is rare that the incumbent president loses an election in some African countries.

The people who fought for independence, for self-determination, have died in jails made by their leaders who, during colonial times, were fellow African freedom-fighters, although some post-colonial African leaders were collaborators with colonial rulers. What Barnnet states is descriptive of the situation in many post-independent African countries:

> Unfortunately . . . Kenya has unmistakably entered the path of neocolonial accommodation. The Kenyatta regime, even before the flag-waving independence ceremony of 12 December 1963, had embarked on a course of self-aggrandizing opportunism and blatant disregard for the peasant and worker masses of Kenya. Virtually every warning contained in this article, every "pitfall of national consciousness" Fanon cautioned against in his *Wretched of the Earth*, has been succumbed to in a Kenya which today is the very antithesis of that creative and developing socialist nation hoped for by radical Kenyans in 1961. Leaders of integrity and dedicated to serving the interests of the masses, men such as Pio Gama Pinto, Bildad Kaggia, and Oginga Odinga, have been assassinated, deported, imprisoned or harassed and intimidated into silence and accommodation. Kenya is today a police state run by a mafia-like clique of self-serving politicians-cum-businessmen. Jomo Kenyatta, two-time betrayer of the Kenya masses (in 1953–4 at Kapenguria and 1962–63), largest African landowner in Kenya, leader of the new Black bourgeoisie and of the corrupt bureaucratic bourgeoisie which comprises the government, was described to me in 1962 by Pio Pinto—then editor of *Sauti ya Mwafrica* and a top Kenyatta advisor—as simply an "amoral man." Pinto was assassinated by the regime on 24 February 1965 and Kenya has yet to replace him.[11]

---

11. Barnett, *Life Histories from the Revolution* (#1), 9.

The Area of African Theology Is an African Social and Historical Context

After independence in many nations of Africa, Christian churches had to redefine themselves. The colonial power was no more—or so it was thought. The Church had to make it understandable that their mission was spiritual as well as promoting human well-being through hospitals and schools. Even after independence, when political mismanagement, embezzlement of public funds, and nepotism, among other ills, had crippled and reduced living standards to squalid level and some governments could not even provide basic services, some churches, especially in their leaders, remained silent. I once heard a president known for his corruption and bad governance in an African country praising the local archbishop for his silence and humility and asking other church leaders who regularly spoke against the evils committed by the head of the state government to be like the archbishop. Unfortunately for that president, from that moment on the archbishop joined the other church leaders in speaking out against the abuses of power by his government.

With independence, many African nations forgot what their main goal was: the freedom and well-being of their people. In some countries the new African leaders were just a replacement of the old colonial masters because they continued with oppression and exploitation. This is usually referred to as neo-colonialism. On neo-colonialism in Namibia, Zephania Kameeta states:

> This tragic phenomenon arises when the oppressed of yesterday—after their victory—become today's oppressors. They forget that the struggle for liberation doesn't end with the day of independence. Instead of serving and giving their lives to redeem the people, they want to be served and worshipped, and even take the lives of their people, so that they can live in luxury. The Lord has chosen his church to be a living witness in such situations, and to proclaim with her existence the new community in him.[12]

Even after independence, African nations continued the struggle or searching for an identity that was genuinely African and at the same time develop political and social structures that were African in nature. Mboya has written:

> Deep down in the mind of every African nationalist there are echoes of the past. On the one hand, there is the echo of the past African world with its ideals, values, and cosmological ideas—

---

12. Kameeta, *Why, O Lord?*, 7.

the past that the African has lost touch with due to the interposition of colonial rule. We are seeking an integration with all that is good and constructive about this past in order to salvage our personality and to find a foundation on which to build our own institutions. On the other hand, there is the recent past of colonial rule, littered with memories of colonial past and to use it as an instrument of contact with the rest of the world.[13]

Mboya advocates for a break between the colonial way of government and the post-independence context. He calls for the development of a genuine African system of government. He sees a good political system as connected with a good economic climate. He states:

Under colonial rule, some economic structures have emerged in our countries which are not suitable and which must either be changed or considerably modified. I think the system of relations between workers and employers in Africa is one of these. Wage-earning in Africa is already a strongly based institution; there are millions of Africans who have no other means of livelihood. Like other workers, these Africans expect that wage-earning will prove human and gratifying. As workers and citizens they expect the same respect accorded to other citizens. They want to feel that they are integral part of industry, doing something meaningful and valuable for the country; they want security in employment, and above all they want dignity accorded to their labour. They want to be consulted on all matters which affect them.[14]

Unfortunately, the oppression of the masses by some governments continues in the new millennium. Koigi Wamwere, a former member of Parliament for Subukia, Kenya, states:

Without a doubt the genesis of Parliament's problems lies in its own history and as a creature of British colonialism. In contradiction to the spirit of its motto, throughout the colonial period, Parliament promoted the unjust government of white settlers and the welfare of a tiny minority of white settlers at the expense of majority Africans. Indeed Legico as Parliament was then called was an integral and crucial part of the colonial machine of crushing Africans. After independence the color of MPs changed but not the primary purpose of Parliament. To make sure it perpetrates, perpetuates and legally justifies oppression and exploitation

13. Mboya, "Keynote Address: Tensions in African Development," 26.
14. Ibid., 28.

of masses Parliament has itself been yoked to five millstones that must be smashed to liberate and make it a servant of the people.[15]

Although Kenya has never been subjected to military rule, it is a good example of a place where post-colonial leaders, some whom were collaborators with colonialists, have oppressed their fellow citizens. Civil dictatorship was entrenched in the post-independent Kenya. For example, in the early 1990s, Kenya was forced by foreign financial donors to allow multi-party system of government. The opposition (those who called for multi-party government) was jailed and detained without appearing in court. Only through the call by donors and the threat to withhold financial aid did the government change the controversial Section 2A of the Constitution that made Kenya *de jure* a single-party state. I know this because I lived through it in Kenya.

In many post-independence countries of Africa, the Church did not want to repeat its silence during colonial times. Many clergymen and women were in the fore-front calling for change and respect of human rights. Some examples are Bishop Desmond Tutu of South Africa and the Kenyan Anglican Bishop Alexander Kipsang Muge, who died in a road crash under mysterious circumstances. Even without stipulating or advocating a theological method, various church leaders and the Christian faithful condemned abuses of human rights simply because it is wrong and against human dignity. The motivation of the Christian faith and gospel is also part and parcel of the African churches' cry for justice.

Democracy, as a form of government, is still very young in many countries of Africa. Although democracy as a form of government is not without some shortcomings, such as the oppression of minorities, an African theology should promote a consciousness in the people in order that all people participate in the choice of government and the issues relevant in building a just and stable society. For this, religion and state in Africa have to work together for nation-building. This collaboration requires religions to embrace a teaching role in their respective societies and the state to help protect the freedom to practice religion. Nation-building is the work of all. Christians themselves are citizens in their respective countries and therefore, their participation in helping bring about a peaceful and just society constitutes a vocation given by God.

---

15. Wamwere, "Parliament in Dire Need of Urgent Reforms."

Factors Contributing to the Cultural and Historical Change in an African Context

From the above, African history can be described as transitory in nature. There are changes happening from cultural, social, political, and economic perspectives. In this section, I consider the various factors that have led to these changes in an African context and their theological implications. They include education, poverty and related issues, and the importance of African religious diversity in conflict resolutions.

Education as a Tool for Cultural and Historical Change

Formal education has played a major role in the cultural transformations of Africa. Through formal education, people become exposed to other forms of knowledge that broaden their worldviews. There is a tremendous difference in worldviews between a person who has gone through formal schooling and one who has not. The majority of African people today have had some formal education. Through education they speak foreign languages, such as English and French. Though African people have not abandoned completely their traditional culture and customs, education has led to people adopting what would otherwise be referred to as foreign ways of life. For example, Bertha Kang'ongo'i reports that even though modernity has eroded traditional social values in Kenya through formal education and the mass media, the Ameru people still maintain the *Nchuri Ncheke* (council of elders). She recommends the traditional council of elders as one way the country could continually curb the rising insecurity and moral decadence. Among the Ameru people, the *Nchuri Ncheke* is presided over by the *mugwe* (overseer) who today is symbolic of the changes affecting the Ameru culture and tradition. Kang'ongo'i points out that the *mugwe*, Dr. Gaita Baikiao II, is very well educated, with a doctoral degree in Divinity and Anthropology.[16]

The inevitability of cultural changes affects not just Africans but also millions of people in the world. The concern for a good formal education has replaced some African traditional practices. For example, graduation from school in some communities is esteemed more than undergoing

---

16. Kang'ongo'i, "Visit to Holy House of the Meru Elders."

some rites of passage, such as circumcision. It is from an understanding of the changed historical circumstances that Mboya lamented:

> Perhaps the greatest crisis facing Africa today is the economic one. We face a situation in which millions are undernourished, uneducated, living narrow lives in poor conditions. This alone would be bad enough. What makes it all the more critical is that these same people, our citizens, had high hopes that independence will change everything.[17]

Further, Mboya adds:

> Mention of education should remind us that half of our population in Kenya consists of young people. While we are doing all we can to widen the economic and social horizons of those who are already adult, obviously our main education efforts, in the widest sense, are directed towards this young half of the society who will lead tomorrow.[18]

With education, people develop a need for gainful employment and with it the necessity to develop a career. Before the introduction of schools, the only careers available included looking after domestic animals, hunting wild game, gathering fruits, roots, and other edibles, as well as farming. However, with the introduction of modern "western" ways of life, a professional career has become a way of earning a living and self-enhancement in the African societies. As early as the 1960s, the problem of unemployment was evident in the newly independent nations. Mboya states:

> Unemployment is one of the greatest crises which confronts some newly independent states. The rising expectations which accompany independence cause an accelerated drift to the towns in search of paid employment. Education policies produce an ever-growing number of school-leavers. Stern measures formerly used by the colonial authorities are no longer appropriate or politically acceptable in a democratic society... Urgent and practical policies must be implemented to solve this explosive crisis. Many African countries see part of the answer in rural development.[19]

---

17. Mboya, *The Challenge of Nationhood*, 10.
18. Ibid., 18.
19. Ibid., 15.

Toward the goal of promoting employment capacities, especially for young adults, some churches today offer some opportunities to solve the problem of unemployment through vocational training. Some examples of church-based vocational training are the Don Bosco technical schools in Nairobi, Makuyu, and Embu (all towns in Kenya), and Consolata Missionaries' Sagana Technical College in Sagana, Kenya. These institutions offer technical training to young people with hope that they will easily find employment or start their own workshops.

It is to these changed cultural settings that African theology and Christian life has to address. The issues that concern African people are similar to those that concern people elsewhere in the world. Issues such as education, health, employment, and security concern human living in any society. Is it necessary to go back to Africa's past to answer questions on human living in contemporary Africa? The answer is yes and no. Yes, because we want to understand where we are coming from and how we can build a solid foundation. And no, because some traditions have become extinct since some cultural practices have died and others have been born. For example, in some traditional African societies, some ethnic groups required the killing of a vicious animal like a lion or leopard as part of initiation into adulthood. Today killing an animal illegally is considered poaching and is punishable by law, although some Maasai people of Kenya and Tanzania still require this initiation.

Many people today in African societies are concerned with improving their lot in life. Today the major route to improving one's life is by getting a good education. Parents want their children to go through school in order to do well in life. However, it is not always possible to get a good education in many parts of Africa. Some people cannot afford to pay for their education. In some places, there are not even any good schools. There is a need, therefore, for an education system that is integrally African as well as addressed to issues in African living today. Inculturation should not only focus on religious issues but also other areas of life. For example, why is an African student taught in a school in Africa using a foreign language? Or why should African scholars write in foreign languages like English, Portuguese, French, and German? Theology as well as religion should help people find solutions to issues concerning human living in society.

The Area of African Theology Is an African Social and Historical Context

Poverty and Related Issues

Poverty is dehumanizing. It reduces the dignity of a people by making them live under conditions that diminish general well being. In contemporary Africa there are problems in health care and nutrition, education, and good social life, as well as economic disadvantages and people not fully participating in political self-determination. It is disheartening to see, hear, and read about extreme suffering caused by poverty in many African regions. Considering all the resources in Africa (oil, various minerals, rich agricultural land, and human potential, among others), it is inconceivable why so many people go without proper nourishment, health care, housing, and other necessities of life. Any true theology should not escape treating the issue of poverty and suffering in Africa. Theology has to respond to the situations of alienation and suffering, not only offering hope but also practical suggestions that lead to positive transformation of living conditions. Christian theology especially should be about justice, love, peace, and all the issues that go into defining improved human living in society.

Christian theology in Africa has a vocation to critique conditions that favor the exploitation of one human being by another. The practical goal of theology is to lead to an understanding of human capacity and the accompanying involvement in shaping and bringing forth the common good in a society. It is about people and their daily life. Theology promotes an understanding of humanity and how the Christian message helps give birth to the integral well being or salvation of all people.

Today, especially in major cities in the West, one hears of the so-called experts on African development. However, the main agents of African development are the African people who know what their situation is and are for this reason the best equipped to bring about radical development. Economic development is a major concern in many African countries. Eradication of poverty is the responsibility of the government and all people in any nation or state.

For example, Ali Mazrui argues that life in Africa, especially economic, is motivated either by profits or prestige. With the prestige motive he implies that people, especially in the traditional African setting, are generally concerned with showing their place in societies by holding large weddings, expensive funerals, etc. The prestige motive is concerned with hospitality. He writes, "The trouble with the prestige motive in a multitribal country is that it inevitably leads to nepotism, and sometimes to other forms of corruption. Corruption can sometimes serve a creative purpose in an underdeveloped country, but in general it is something which a government ought to be on guard against. Nepotism and corruption can often stifle efficiency."[20] He adds, "However, there is room also for the more disguised forms of governmental pressure—the self-help schemes and the adventures in human investment. In this case the village-oriented prestige motive can be utilized to advantage—a new school might be built by the village for the village's own prestige."[21] But "With regard to foreign businesses in new states, the profit motive assumes sovereignty all over again. Indeed, only the profit motive can attract foreign investment. While the Government in an African country is busy trying to exploit or control the prestige inducement which is latent in its own people, it has also to appeal to the profit instinct of foreign investors."[22] He argues for the need of planning in the new states, and that to achieve development some changes are needed in traditional societies.[23] Mazrui makes a suggestion for a "planned delay" in some traditional societies to give leaders ample time to gain experience.[24] This is questionable. How long can a suffering people wait for the removal of the causes of their sufferings? However, Mazrui answers, "The concept of 'preparing for planning' is not in any case, a call for governmental inaction."[25]

From a practical perspective, the greatest cause of poverty and suffering is unemployment. People who cannot find meaningful work to earn some money to support themselves and their families are destitute people. Economic development is therefore connected with the availability of gainful employment.

Christian faith and theology should make a contribution by providing alternate ways and means to bring about integral human flourishing in society. Even if Christianity is not identical with any political system, it provides a way of understanding human dignity as created in the image and likeness of God. Many Christian denominations view human beings

---

20. Mazrui, "Is African Development Plannable?" 138.
21. Ibid., 140.
22. Ibid.
23. Ibid., 140–41.
24. Ibid., 141–42.
25. Ibid., 143.

as having an inherent calling to be co-creators with God. Work is one of the ways that people contribute to society and benefit through remuneration in wages and other related benefits. Work, in a special way, is one of the major factors that constitute a person's life. It can be referred to as a human right.

Unfortunately, in many African nations there are so many people who are unemployed or under-employed. There are migrant workers who cannot find employment in their home countries and who move to other countries where chances of employment are presumably better off. There is need for solidarity between the developed countries of the world and the developing or the very poor countries of the world. Dietmar Mieth states:

> The precedence of the claim of the disadvantaged to solidarity has the effect, in the dimension of work and unemployment, that the needs of those people take precedence who are most disadvantaged by the international labour market situation. The principle of solidarity therefore supports the maxim of justice, of seeking the greatest good for the most disadvantaged. This ethical maxim coincides in its turn with the maxim of liberation theology which is described generally as 'option for the poor.' This theological-ethical maxim presupposes, of course, that the first step in the practical conversion in this direction has already been accomplished. Solidarity in the Christian context is not merely a maxim of conviction, but the result of a new praxis which is already at work. Such solidarity is not an imposed moral duty, but the unavoidable answer to the claims of the Christian faith, on the basis of which what is actually humanly self-evident is not only recognizable, but practical.[26]

Nevertheless, Africa should never sacrifice preservation of the natural environment at the altar of capitalistic production. A balance should be maintained between economic development and the conservation of nature (people, wildlife, forests, mountains, etc). All economic development should be sustainable (i.e. to preserve and conserve the environment as we promote economic production in industries, agriculture, mining, etc.). Ultimately, Christianity and other African religions have a major responsibility in promoting good living standards for all people

---

26. Mieth, "Solidarity and the Right to Work," 58.

through motivation as well as through community projects and provision of essential services.

The Wealth of African Religious Diversity Is to Be Seen through Conflict Resolution

Diversity defines the nature of the African continent. There is diversity in race, ethnicity, language, geography, and religion, among others. Africa is not a culturally homogenous continent. Besides the major world religions such as Christianity and Islam, there are many traditional religions in Africa and also people who have no known religious affiliation. Each ethnic group has its religious traditions based on the respective understanding of human existence and the natural world.

African religious diversity is a statement of the need to develop ways for peaceful co-existence. It calls for religious dialogue. Religious pluralism has not received much theological attention in Africa. Many theologians have been concerned with developing theology from and for their respective religious traditions. The Second Vatican Council's "Declaration on the Relation of the Church to Non-Christian Religions" states: "Ever aware of her duty to foster unity and charity among individuals, and even among nations, she reflects at the outset on what men have in common and what tends to promote fellowship among them."[27]

However, the lack of theological interest in religious diversity in Africa is counteracted by the reality of true dialogue by religious leaders and lay people in some communities. An example of religious dialogue is in Kenya where Christian church leaders join their Islamic counterparts to give joint statements on some social and political issues that concern all people at the national level. Or even in families where members belong to different religious affiliation.

There are many conflicts that have devastated and continue to devastate Africa—for example, the conflict in southern Sudan that went on for over twenty years and claimed millions of lives. Unfortunately, in the same Sudan recently a conflict broke out in the Darfur region that has relentlessly killed tens of thousands. In the civil war in Liberia, hundreds of thousands were killed and others rendered homeless. Not far away from Liberia was the despicable maiming and mutilation of children, women, and men in Sierra Leone. The horrendous abduction and raping of

---

27. Flannery, *Nostra Aetate*, No. 1, 738.

children continues in northern Uganda by the rebels of the Lord's Resistance Army led by Joseph Kony.[28] And the unforgettable genocide of 1994 in Rwanda took over 500,000 lives. The list goes on and on. All these are but a few of the tragedies that continue to maim and decimate the African people, and it is ironic because a majority of Africans, especially in many conflict zones, are Christians or members of other religions. The question remains unanswered on the correlation between religion and conflicts in the African context.

Where people co-exist together conflicts are bound to happen. But the most important issue would be how to resolve these conflicts and avoid them escalating to violence or civil wars. The story by the late Mwalimu Julius Nyerere, the former president of Tanzania, describes how conflicts arise when he states:

> By working together, two men can cut and transport a log of wood which is too heavy for either of them alone. With it they can jointly make a canoe large enough to go further away from land than one made by either of the men alone. Through their co-operation each of the men will have increased his power to travel—will have enlarged his effective freedom on the earth. But, at the same time, each of the men has lost his individual freedom in relation to that log. Neither, for example, can decide alone that it would after all be better to use it for building a house, or for firewood. And once the canoe has been made as a result of their joint effort neither of them can take it fishing on his own, nor exchange it for something entirely different—however much he might need the proposed exchange object. Their joint effort has enlarged the freedom of them both; but it has also introduced new possibilities of conflict which did not exist when each of them built a small canoe on his own. [sic][29]

However, Nyerere does believe conflict can be avoided. He does not stop at the indispensability of conflict, but he suggests a way to prevent it from occurring and a way out of it when it occurs. He states, "The only system of law which brings peace is a system which is based on the fundamental human equality of all the people under its suzerainty, and which

---

28. See Kimani, "Uganda's Children of the Night Sucked into an Orgy of Violence."
29. Nyerere, "The Courage of Reconciliation," 267.

aims at reconciling to the greatest possible degree man's conflicting desires for individual freedom and the benefits of communal life."³⁰

African countries have a responsibility to work for peace and resolve conflicts that have been ruining parts of the continent for decades. This has started to happen through organizations such as the African Union (previously the Organization of African Unity), which brings together all the nations in the African continent. For example, in *The East African*, a weekly newspaper published in Nairobi, Kenya, Kevin Kelley makes the following comment:

> The apparent resolution of the 20-year conflict in southern Sudan must be counted as a key success in efforts to bring greater stability to the entire region, say the experts. Just as Kenya serves as a model for democratic elections, the country acts as a "linchpin" in peacemaking initiatives throughout East Africa . . . In addition to the important role Kenya played in ending hostilities in southern Sudan, Nairobi has been instrumental in transporting relief supplies to the Democratic Republic of Congo and in pushing forward the peace process in Somalia.³¹

Besides the political solutions to conflicts, the Christian message and faith can contribute a great deal in conflict resolution. Christians have a mission as peacemakers. The beatitudes come to mind: "Blessed are the peacemakers, for they will be called children of God" (Matt 5:9). The concept of peace implies integral well-being of all people in society. Peace implies harmony in human co-existence.³² The ways and means of Christian conflict resolutions need to be considered and developed, but there is too much silence in African churches concerning conflict resolutions.

The religious contribution to conflict resolution is necessary because many conflicts in Africa have a religious aspect. For example, in northern

---

30. Ibid., 268.

31. Kelly, "Elections." However, the 2007 post-election violence in Kenya caused by a flawed general election indicated the long way the country has to go to achieve democratic maturity.

32. See Jürgen Moltmann's description of peace: "Peace means not only the absence of war but also the overcoming of suffering, anxiety, threat, injustice, and oppression. Peace is the blessed, affirmed, good, splendid life with God, with human beings, and with nature: *Shalom*. It is the commission of Christians to serve this peace in all dimensions of life, to promote it and protect it, but in particular to resist war, the most dangerous form of the lack of peace." (Cited from Moltmann, *Following Jesus Christ in the World Today*, 91).

The Area of African Theology Is an African Social and Historical Context

Nigeria, the conflict between the Muslims and Christians is religious as well as political in nature. In the Nigerian conflict, politics has hijacked religion and used it as a tool for furthering a political agenda: the balance of power in the governing of the country. Instead of conflict between Christians and Muslims, dialogue and peaceful resolution would benefit both sides. The conflicts voice a void in theological thinking and practice because theology and religious life should constitute one harmonious and integrated social life. In the practice of religion, there is a theological foundation and formulation of beliefs and rituals. There should be no separation between belief and practice. The role of the theologian in situations of conflict should be to critique the situation and promote a sound theological understanding, and thereby providing some alternatives to violence: dialogue leading to peaceful co-existence.

In situations of human conflict, whether religious or political, a task is inherent for African theological study to promote dialogue between religious groupings as well as ethnic groups. Theology should be a means to dialogue as well as dialogue itself. By omission, in cases of conflict, silence in Christian churches or even Islamic mosques, or in any religious group for that matter, can mean that the members approve the violence meted upon the people.

Conclusion

The chapter evaluates the changed African historical and social contexts and argues that in these changed situations consists the task of African theologies. The Africa of the past is gone, and new realities have emerged. However, historical continuity in an African context cannot be denied, but it is also important to remember that dwelling in the past does not do justice to African contemporary contexts. In summary, the chapter sets a foundation for a re-defining of African theologies. The next chapter deals with the social nature of the Christian faith and its relevance in an African historical context.

2

The Social Nature of the Christian Faith and the African Historical Context

THE SOCIAL NATURE OF Christianity as a religion is seen in the fact that it is a faith lived by human beings in community. Furthermore, any Christian community is always a part of its respective society. There is no way Christians can live and not engage the larger society as citizens. In this section, without denying the social role of other world religions, Christian faith is viewed as capable of bringing transformation in a society. Social issues affecting the African continent, as discussed in the previous section, are also in the domain of the Christian faith, and therefore a Christian community can help achieve a just and equitable society. The Christian gospel and faith can motivate believers to work for justice, peace, and the common good, leading to a Christian community becoming a community of liberation.

PART ONE

The Redeeming or Liberating Nature of the Christian Faith

The central teaching of the Christian faith is that, through Jesus Christ, God has redeemed the world. The redemption brought about by Jesus Christ is understood to include all human beings and all of creation. Hence, St. Paul, one of the first and greatest Christian missionaries in the early church, stated: "We know that all creation is groaning in labor pains even until now; and not only that, but we ourselves, who have the firstfruits of the Spirit, we also groan within ourselves as we wait for adoption, the redemption of our bodies" (Rom 8:22–23). The redemption of human beings in Christianity is understood in an integral way to include the whole human person, body and soul.

The Social Nature of the Christian Faith

In theological scholarship, the concepts of redemption and liberation have been used interchangeably. Redemption and liberation mean one and the same thing—that is, the integral well-being of the human person. Hence, the attempt to separate redemption from liberation would only be in the mind and devoid of foundation in the gospel of Jesus Christ. The kingdom proclaimed by Jesus is addressed to the well-being of the whole human person (Luke 4:17b–19; cf. Isa 40:1–5, 9–11).

Understanding the liberating nature of Christianity calls upon an understanding of the new being brought about by faith in Jesus Christ. It is the person who lives in the new life of the spirit who goes out guided by that spirit to work for justice, love, and peace in society. However, Christian liberation theology can be accused of making a mistake of limiting the work of liberation to human effort to the exclusion of the grace of God or the spirit of God. Grace in Christian teaching refers, in a special way, to God's presence in a believer. This presence is understood to move a believer to build God's kingdom on earth, especially through works of justice and charity. A Christian faithful would lament that there is great emphasis on the human power in liberation theology to the exclusion of the spiritual life of faith in Jesus Christ.[1] This might be conceived of as leading to a doctrinal problem because Jesus Christ is viewed like any other historical figure who motivates by example, other than God, who is present in the hearts and minds of the people working for justice and peace in the world.

From the above, the struggle for human liberation can be said to be perennial everywhere, and especially in Africa, where dehumanizing factors of poverty, disease, and oppression need be eradicated. The fight against colonialism and neo-colonialism in Africa was referred to as the struggle for liberation. It can therefore be argued that liberation theology in an African context does not bring forth a new reality but gives a name to African struggles. Liberation in African Christianity should highlight the role of the Christian faith in helping to transform situations of alienation in the larger society. What is new in liberation theology in Africa is that it can provide a voice, a medium of expression, to the otherwise silent Christian churches. Liberation theology articulates the social role of Christian teachings. Africa's history is a history of liberation. The struggle for political independence comes to mind. Even before independence

---

1. See J. Ratzinger's critique of liberation theology in "Instruction on Certain Aspects of the 'Theology of Liberation.'"

movements and the coming of colonial rule, and for that matter, the coming of Christianity, Africans struggled to remain free and prosperous as ethnic groups. Prosperity was seen to be a result of right living as well as a people's self-determination, by protecting their land from "outsiders" (other ethnic groups and colonialists) and by hard work.

However, the concern for human well-being is not limited to Christianity, Islam, or the traditional religions of Africa. It is a human concern present in all people, be they in politics, economics, or any other profession. Julius Nyerere, in a pamphlet published in 1958, states:

> What is the origin of the right to possess wealth? What prompts a person into declaring anything to be "mine"? From where does a man derive the right to possess something, and to refuse the whole world this right of ownership? This right originates from only one factor; the fact that man is nobody's property. He owns himself and cannot be someone else's possession. So, whenever he uses his intellect, his health and his ability to make anything, that thing becomes his property . . . Land is a free gift from God to all His living things to be used now and in the future.[2]

Nyerere argues that ownership, especially of land, is by temporary tenancy. I own it today and in the future leave it to somebody else. Notably, Nyerere came to be opposed to the freehold ownership of land because he thought it would lead to poor Tanzanians becoming landless after selling their land to foreigners and wealthy people.[3] He supported leasehold ownership where owners paid small land rents.

The study of theology has also to concern itself with the good life (*eu zen*). The commandment to love God and love one's neighbor in Christianity promotes good relationships in human living. The people in community are neighbors, and they are viewed as connected with God. Christian faith is not practiced outside society. Christians have a duty to contribute to the good life, which is also the concern of the political setup of any society. However, unnecessary entanglements of religion and politics have been historically deleterious, especially in medieval Europe and even in some contemporary theocratic nations. In a pluralistic state, religion and politics, though influencing each other, should be separate. But the concern of good human living in society makes it a duty for theol-

---

2. Nyerere, "National Property," 53.
3. Ibid., 54–5.

The Social Nature of the Christian Faith

ogy to engage itself in issues in society that are the concern of all people, irrespective of their faith affiliation. In a chapter entitled "Demystifying Martin and Malcom," James Cone states:

> The radical Martin was also an anti-war activist and a challenger of the economic order. He called racism, war, and poverty the three great evils of his time. Opposition to the war in Vietnam and to poverty and racism at home and abroad became Martin's major obsession as he proclaimed God's judgment upon America. His opposition was more than just a political protest. It was a theological and prophetic "condemnation of America."[4]

Liberation theology can awaken the Christian churches in Africa. The churches should concern themselves with the well being of all people in their societies; otherwise they risk becoming irrelevant. Church relevance in society involves working to change situations of suffering and oppression to ones of integral human flourishing. Unfortunately, some churches in history have supported systems of oppression, thereby becoming agents of pain and suffering. Allan Boesak, the anti-apartheid activist from South Africa, states:

> Through the centuries the churches have often sided with the oppressors in the name of law and order. The question now is whether the churches shall repeat the mistakes of the past, or would they at last begin to preach the gospel as it relates to the total meaning of history revealed in Christ. This recovery of the mission of the church requires a concern for identification with the peoples who are involved in the revolutionary struggles to change existing power structures. This approach presupposes that the work of Christ and his kingdom is discernible in the secular, social, and political revolutions of our time and that the church's function is to discern it and to witness to it and to participate in God's work in changing the world.[5]

From the teachings of Christ, the churches have a mission to be outstanding witnesses to freedom.[6] Any church that would support and

4. Cone, *Risks of Faith*, 101.
5. Boesak, *Farewell to Innocence*, 83.
6. See what Jürgen Moltmann writes on the danger of Christians not involving themselves in what is happening in the world: "So just as the Anabaptists stand in danger of pulling themselves back out of the world quietistically and without criticism, so the Lutherans stand in danger of going along with the world as it is and cooperating without criticism. The "silent ones in the land" and the "pious state underlings" thus in the end

justify oppression does not in essence represent the saving message of Jesus Christ. Jesus identified with the poor and the downtrodden. In turn, churches have a duty to be the voice to the voiceless. Evidently, Christianity has a message that is relevant in helping bring forth a social order where human dignity is respected. Witnessing to a just social order is part of Jesus' proclamation of God's kingdom (Mark 1:15).

PART TWO

The Role of Christianity in Social Transformation

The Christian message is modeled on the teachings of Jesus Christ. John 10:10–11 sums up the teachings of Christ thus: "I came so that they might have life and have it more abundantly. I am the good shepherd. A good shepherd lays down his life for the sheep." The basic role of Christianity is the promotion of human living, both spiritually and physically. Like Christ, Christians are to have mercy for the poor or the destitute: to feed the hungry, to offer drink to the thirsty, to clothe the naked, to visit the sick and the prisoners, etc. All these will be the basis for the final judgment (Matt 25:31–46).

From the time Christian missionaries went to Africa, Christianity has been connected with the promotion of education and healthcare.[7] Christian churches have been at the forefront in the promotion of economic, social, and cultural life through education programs in schools and churches. The parishes in African dioceses are the centers of spiritual, social, and developmental activities. Members of the church, clergy and lay people alike, have been known to speak out against abuses of human rights.

In a parish in Africa, the main concern should be the promotion of the integral well being of the people—that is, spiritual and physical needs, not just a theological or pastoral method. Human well-being is the center of Christian life. Unfortunately, there is so much theoretical analysis about liberation and much less transformative action; this contradicts the understanding of praxis in liberation theology. The concern is not the making of rules and regulations but helping people realize true freedom of the children of God. The praxis of the Christian gospel should not be

---

have little to contribute to peace and justice in economics and politics in the world" (Moltmann, *Following Jesus Christ in the World Today,* 90).

7. Isichei, *A History of Christianity in Africa,* 74–97.

The Social Nature of the Christian Faith

complicated. Its simplicity should be appreciated. There are times the law of the Church can be seen to hinder the spontaneity of love taught by Jesus Christ in the gospels.[8] The gospel of Matthew is instructive: "Come to me, all you who labor and are burdened, and I will give you rest. Take my yoke upon you and learn from me, for I am meek and humble of heart; and you will find rest for yourselves. For my yoke is easy, and my burden light" (Matt 11:28–30). The task of liberation is simple and yet complex. Simple activity such as to satisfy the needs of a poor or sick or a hungry person by providing food, medicine, and clothing (basic necessities) constitute the Christian praxis (action). Also, the complex activities that go to the root cause of the problem are included in the Christian praxis, such as asking the deeper questions of why the poor are poor. Elimination of the factors that lead to poverty and disease requires a radical systemic change (revolution). Sometimes a society has to destroy a system or a socio-economic structure in order to build a new and a better one.

Christian Faith and Social Issues

Christian faith provides a foundation for working to change and eliminate the root causes of poverty, suffering, and oppression. The Christian call to conversion can be understood both privately and publicly. It is individual human beings who hear the call to conversion from the gospel of Christ, and the community of believers in Christ can give a witness to love in a society, thereby bringing about social change. In themselves, properly understood, Christian teachings provide a good foundation for social living. However, there should be awareness that an uncritical fundamentalism can be a danger to social harmony and progress.

Consequently, Christian teaching provides a worldview to deal with social issues. Appealing to non-Christian philosophical and political thought in the history of Christian social thought can be viewed as having both positive and negative implications. It is positive because it provides a foundation to show the validity of Christian social thought outside the Christian churches and thereby appeal to non-Christian people. But it can be viewed as negative in the sense that it can be seen to promote the idea that the Christian gospel is not adequate in itself and needs the validation of other philosophical or thought systems. Besides being a way of life, Christianity provides a way of thinking and being in the world. However,

---

8. Gutiérrez, *Theology of Liberation*, 6–11.

the Christian teachings can be misused to justify unjust and oppressive social systems. For example, Peter Katjavivi states:

> Namibians have had to face the combined force of Afrikaner-controlled church and state and the spread of Christian nationalist philosophy through the education system, with its emphasis on preparing different races for their different roles in apartheid society. The symbol of Afrikaner domination *is "Die Boer met sy Bybel en sy Röer"* (The Boer with his *Bible* and rifle). A vital part of the nationalist struggle has been the assertion of black consciousness and dignity. Liberation theology has developed as an important part of this struggle for a means of greater self-awareness and self-esteem, and of liberation from a state of poverty, suffering, humiliation, exploitation and family disintegration.[9]

Nonetheless, Christian teachings can borrow and apply what is good in other philosophical systems while working to eliminate what is oppressive and against human dignity as such. As an example, despite the socialist and communist systems' denial and control of individual self-deliberation and freedom, liberation theology as a theological method can be said to appeal to Marxist materialist thought in its teaching on praxis and social transformation. Nevertheless, the message of theology of liberation could be sufficiently understood and applied in a concrete situation without appealing to the Marxist materialistic interpretation of society. The gospels present the teaching of Jesus Christ, who was concerned with the poor, the sick, the oppressed, and most of all, all humanity under the yoke of sin. How about the early Christian community in Jerusalem who shared all their material possessions with one another (Acts 2:42–47)? Liberation or salvation is the central message in the Christian gospel. For Christianity to be meaningful, it has to address issues in social justice and bring about social transformation. Gustavo Gutiérrez is among the most-known advocates of the theology of liberation.

Generally, the theology of liberation can be said to have demonstrated the possibility of Christian involvement with issues in the political and social domain. However, the praxis advocated by liberation theologians can also be criticized for not providing a political and social system that can be put into concrete practice in a particular society. The emphasis on praxis can ironically be turned into a theory that remains in the mind with no real social action happening on the ground. It is not enough to

---

9. Katjavivi, "The Role of the Church in the Struggle for Independence," 22.

The Social Nature of the Christian Faith

talk about praxis. Praxis implies social action, and therefore, to write or talk about it with no social transformative action is a contradiction in terms. The question remains of how effective a theologian of liberation is in the social milieu. I do not deny the contribution liberation theologians have in their respective societies, but I am emphasizing that liberation theology has to deal with a concrete historical setting. Liberation theology has to have a hands-on approach to social issues if it is not to remain in academia as any other theory divorced from practical action. Making people aware that they can do something about their social woes, the causes of their situation of oppression and alienation, and that the people themselves have the power to bring about transformation is itself a part and parcel of the process of social praxis. Unfortunately, talk on liberation theology is mostly heard and developed in academia.

In a fundamental way, Christian thought has a message to offer to all sectors of human living—political, social, and economic. Marcus Borg writes of a dream of God as connected with a politics of compassion.[10] Borg holds that "... a politics of compassion is not a particular set of specific economic and social policies but a social vision that is to affect our political thinking."[11] The task of politics is to help bring about good life in society. Christian faith in God also has a role to play in realizing the good life in society. However, in a more integral way, Christian teachings have a way of making human flourishing possible. The connection between health care, education, and evangelization in the work of nineteenth- and twentieth-century missionaries in Africa is a good example. Hence, one can say that faith in God shapes a people's outlook on life. A people's social environment and their understanding of the world around them shapes their religious and ethical life. For example, in medieval times, usury was forbidden because in the economic situation of the time it was viewed as unjustified profiteering.

To believe in Jesus is to follow in his footsteps. Jesus lived and helped the poor in his everyday life. He proclaimed liberty to the captives and cured those who were sick. Jesus proclaimed the kingdom of God, a kingdom of peace and justice. In the person of Jesus, God is believed to have visited his people. He is the sun of justice. The people who became believers in the early church in the first and second century AD, sold everything

---

10. Borg, *The God We Never Knew*, 132–36.
11. Ibid., 150.

and brought it to the community (Acts 2:42–47). The social teaching of the Roman Catholic Church or the Protestant churches' "social gospel" is based on the kingdom of God proclaimed by Jesus. Pope Leo XIII wrote the encyclical *Rerum Novarum* (*On the Condition of Workers*).[12] *Rerum Novarum* addressed the deplorable situation of the workers that came about with industrial revolution. The encyclical *Quadragesimo Anno* came at the celebration of the fortieth anniversary of *Rerum Novarum*. Other papal encyclicals, such as *Populorum Progressio* and *Pacem in Terris,* dealt with the questions of development and the cold war arms race.

Religion has a role in addressing the general and social life of people in society. It was Karl Marx who said that religion is the "opiate of the masses." Religion could be an "opiate" if it does not address the issues that concern people in any historical situation. Marx's understanding of history was a materialistic interpretation of society in which the rich factory and estate owners (the bourgeoisie) oppressed the poor masses. His critique and call for change was justified. A Christian understanding of the world and humanity should embrace an integral view where the physical (material) and spiritual dimensions of existence are conceived to form one undivided whole.

Since religion, or Christianity for that matter, has a role to play in the life of people in society, then there has to be some involvement in the policy-making structure of any particular society. Religious involvement in political life is a controversial issue in many places in the world. Modernity emphasized the separation of religion and state. This separation, which is highly emphasized in the contemporary world, has a historical background in the experience of abuse of the secular powers by the religious leaders and vice versa. This has been a problem since Emperor Constantine embraced Christianity in the Roman Empire.

Christians as citizens of any given state and as taxpayers have a moral obligation to work for economic accountability and social responsibility. Christian participation in social and political life is a God-given responsibility. It is a Christian duty to work for good governance in religious and socio-political issues. What determines people's political affiliations? Does Christian faith affect political thinking? In either case, religious people should not impose upon other people their religious views. The social order should not be equated with a sectarian view of God's will.

12. For a detailed listing of documents on Catholic social teachings see O'Brien and Shannon, *Catholic Social Thought Documentary Heritage.*

The Social Nature of the Christian Faith

Any society should be able to embrace diversity of opinions and beliefs. Separation of religion and state is a defining issue of modern nations, especially in the West.

Further, it is not easy to distinguish when a Christian is acting as a citizen or acting in the capacity of what I call "a faith-person." The preceding point to the problem of what Borg calls separating life into: (i) a private realm of religion and (ii) a public realm of economics and politics.[13] St. Augustine of Hippo had a dual view of what was worldly and what was heavenly. He wrote of the two cities, the heavenly city and the worldly (earthly) city. The two cities, according to Augustine, had two separate governments. The heavenly was governed by God's will, while human desires and wants controlled the earthly city. The two cities in Augustine's thought are two distinct kingdoms.[14] Nonetheless, the two cities (or kingdoms) theory is not without criticism. Jürgen Moltmann states:

> The two kingdoms doctrine presents the gospel of Christ within an apocalyptic eschatology of the ongoing battle between the kingdom of God and the kingdom of the devil. This apocalyptic eschatology comes from the Old Testament; it was not developed from New Testament Christology. The two kingdoms doctrine paints Christology into the framework of this apocalyptic eschatology. Is that correct? Must not the gospel of Jesus Christ begin from the resurrection of Christ and God's victory over the power of evil in the cross? Apocalyptic eschatology understands Christ from within the world-historical struggle of God against evil, but it fails to understand history and the end of history from the viewpoint of Christ's victory.[15]

Consequently, the way people think about God can have an effect in the kind of society they help or don't help build. A fanatical religious domination can lead to a religiously and politically oppressed nation. Examples are the Taliban in Afghanistan and the fundamentalist Christian rebels of the "former catechist" Joseph Kony in Uganda who fights to take over the Ugandan government and fashion one of their own guided by the Ten Commandments. However, it should be stressed that good thinking about God by people can lead to a transformed and improved social

---

13. Borg, *The God We Never Knew*, 132.
14. See Augustine, "The Compatibility of Christianity and Politics," 202–12.
15. Moltmann, *Following Jesus Christ in the World Today*, 37.

order.[16] Religious values can help bring about the good life in the sociopolitical setting.

Besides politics, there is a relationship between religion and culture in human history. For example, renaissance art (or painting) reflects a religion centered on the goodness and beauty of humanity or the glorious nature of the human body. Also, in the Old Testament the "dream of God" of the Israelites, as Borg calls it, was connected to their social and political vision. A good religious life should always have the task of fighting against inequities and oppressions and working for justice in society. Borg refers to the biblical *shalom* as meaning more than the absence of war but rather a situation of peace and tranquility, where all have food and drink, where the lion and the deer can lie down together in peace.[17]

Ultimately, any religion should be watchful not to act as a justifying cause for corruption in society. Christianity, most of all, should challenge structures in society that promote poverty and suffering. A religion that legitimizes a corrupt social order is a sin that cries to the heavens. Unfortunately, in some countries under authoritarian regimes there are state-sponsored churches that are part of corrupt systems.

The Motivation of Love in the Christian Social Transformation

There is need for a theological method that provides a way to achieve a radical transformation of a society. A method is important since it provides guidelines, but the main concern is the spontaneous action inspired by the Christian gospel and faith. A poor and hungry person would not need to know, for example, whether the theology of liberation is being applied when she or he is provided with food or some seed for sowing in his or her family farm. The issue is not one of method but one of being attentive, like Jesus, to the cry of the sick and the needy. The motivation of love is sufficient in the Christian life, and it is founded on the teachings of Jesus Christ in the gospels and the life of the community. However, the Christian gospel is inseparable from human reasoning because it is understood and lived by human persons. The dictates of the gospel are reasonable but can also help open up new horizons in the human power of reason. The preceding applies especially to a person who professes religious faith.

16. Borg, 133.
17. Ibid., 134.

The Social Nature of the Christian Faith

In dealing with issues of human wellbeing, the spontaneity of love is called upon. Christian faith is not inactive but should move people into good deeds. Faith becomes the motivating force for a believer in Christ to break the shell of paralysis and do something to change situations of suffering and desperation. James 2:14–17 reads:

> What good is it, my brothers, if someone says he has faith but does not have works? Can that faith save him? If a brother or sister has nothing to wear and has no food for the day, and one of you says to them, "Go in peace, keep warm, and eat well," but you do not give them the necessities of the body, what good is it? So also faith of itself, if it does not have works, is dead.

The Christian teaching on love can be referred to as the basic principle of religious and social transformation. Love is the essence of Christian living. The New Testament teaches that God is love. Love is what should always motivate Christian living. Knowing that one is loved by the caring and compassionate God is in itself a call for a Christian to love others. Christian love is active. It is a way of life. Love cannot be defined as such; it can only be described through actions and signs of good will. To love another person is to wish him or her good as well as to do anything that makes his or her life integrally good.

The love of God and neighbor is the basic teaching of Christianity in the New Testament. Jesus summed up the commandments of God as love of God and neighbor (Matt 22:34–40). Hence, the love of God and neighbor should be the principal source of motivation for a Christian in society. Love challenges an individual person to help the neighbor. It does not require a theological system enumerating the reasons for and against working for a just social order. It is unconditional and can act as the basic instinct in the radical change of society. It is the principle of conversion. But love cannot be enforced by the state since the law is the foundation of the state and love goes beyond any law or state. However, the law based on the will of the people in a nation or state can also express love by its requirements. In Christian living, love is viewed as the basic principle. Theology is concerned with the study of human relationships and God. It is critical inquiry and analyses aimed at understanding human living in the world. Further, the Christian doctrine of the Holy Trinity provides the core in the study of God, who is love.

Trinitarian Doctrine as the Basis for Social Action

Christian faith is summed up in the teaching that God is the loving trinity of persons. The Christian mystery of God is formulated in the doctrine of the Most Holy Trinity. From the economy of salvation, God is known as the Holy Trinity. The economy of salvation refers to God's intervention in history to save his people. "The entire Christian economy of salvation is thus a single mystery that can be summed up in one sentence: through Jesus Christ and in the Holy Spirit God is the salvation of man."[18] The communion of love in the three persons yet one God provides a basis for understanding the human community. Love is the building block of the human community. For example, married partners and their children are believed to form a family based on the foundation of the love Jesus Christ has for his Church (Eph 5:25–30).

Trinitarian faith is that in the one God are three persons: Father, Son, and the Holy Spirit. Walter Kasper has argued for the human concern for unity of reality as a preparation to the thinking of the trinity and the oneness of God. For example, Kasper writes: "With the philosophy of Neo-Platonism and Thomas one must say that unity as a transcendental predicate of being applies analogously and not univocally to the various spheres of being."[19] However, Kasper cautiously points out that the Christian doctrine of the Trinity is not to be derived from non-scriptural myths and religions. Unity in the trinity, according to Christianity, is "not a cosmological problem that embraces both God and the world, but strictly a theological and even intra-divine problem."[20] The oneness of God is a biblical teaching. "The oneness of the biblical God shows itself initially only in the fact that Yahweh is superior to other gods; he makes an exclusive claim and shows himself a jealous God who will suffer no other gods besides himself (Ex 20:3ff.; Deut 5:7)."[21]

The Trinity is a Christian teaching on the mystery of God. Human concern for unity can be seen, for example, in the philosophical postulation of being as a way of showing the unity of reality. Western theology has used classical philosophy and tradition in the inquiry on the question of God. God came to be viewed as the answer to human existential

18. Kasper, *The God of Jesus Christ*, 270.
19. Ibid., 236.
20. Ibid., 237.
21. Ibid., 238.

concerns. A theological study of God was conceived as leading to an understanding of the true nature of human personality. The transcendental nature of the human subject or person is understood as the one making human freedom possible (Karl Rahner).

Ultimate freedom is conceived of as possible in God alone, and the broad horizons of human freedom are understood from the point of view of the divine freedom. Hence, human freedom is thought of as a participation in divine freedom. God is the being that exists in itself (i.e., independently of any other and therefore the absolutely free being). The definition of God's essence in the horizon of freedom shows the importance of understanding the uniqueness of the human person (individuality). In the human person, there is tension between individuality and unlimited openness to the whole of reality. The human person can get no satisfaction in anything finite, and for this reason it is argued that human freedom points to God.[22] God is defined as perfect freedom. The Bible presents God as father and thereby shows that personality necessarily means relationality. We realize ourselves in relationship, and human fulfillment is possible through relationship. The category of person is applied to God only by analogy. God is conceived as incomparably higher than anything present in human personality.[23]

Mark 1:15 provides a summary of Jesus' teaching and ministry. The proclamation of the Kingdom of God is the central message of Jesus. According to Kasper, "Jesus is able to rediscover the world as God's creation and proclaim God as Lord of all reality."[24] Jesus embodies God's action in the world. However, God's action does not eliminate human action—on the contrary, it makes human action possible and free. The Kingdom of God, according to Jesus, is not the sign of judgment but is a sign of grace, forgiveness, mercy, and love. Jesus linked his cause, the kingdom, with his own person.[25] The idea of self-emptying (*kenosis*) explains the fact that the Son of God took a human form.[26]

From the above, the mystery of God is viewed as making it possible to understand human beings as inter-relational. Human persons are

22. Ibid., 154.
23. Ibid., 155–56.
24. Ibid., 167–68.
25. Ibid., 168.
26. Ibid., 176.

understood as related to God and to other human beings and the world. Basically, this relationship between human persons and with God can be described as one of love and interdependence.

The Doctrine of the Holy Trinity as Basis for Christian Social Ethics

The Christian doctrine of God in no uncertain terms holds that God is a personal God. The personal nature of God points to the possibility of communication within the one God and also communication with human persons in the world. In the Holy Trinity there is the community of persons: the Father, the Son, and the Holy Spirit. As seen before, the personal nature of God is love. The love of God suggests that God is capable of relationship with other persons. Further, the doctrine of the Holy Trinity suggests the reality of communion in the one God, and this communion in God can be viewed as a basis for building communion in human living. The human community, specifically the Christian community, has its connection to the faith in community in the Holy Trinity.

Understanding the personal nature of the Holy Trinity has social implications for the Christian faithful. Daniel Migliore states:

> Christian social ethics is thus grounded in Trinitarian theology. The Christian hope for peace with justice and freedom in community among peoples of diverse cultures, races, and gender corresponds to the Trinitarian logic of God. Confession of the triune God radically calls in question all totalitarianisms that deny the freedom and rights of all people and resists all idolatrous individualisms that subvert the common welfare. The doctrine of the Trinity seeks to describe God's "being in love" as the source of all genuine community, beyond all sexism, racism, and classism. Trinitarian theology, when it rightly understands its own depth grammar, offers a profoundly relational and communal view both of God and of life created and redeemed by God.[27]

In the preceding, Christian trinitarian faith can be said to have an inherent praxis. To believe in the God who is love and who out of love created the heavens and the earth, human beings, and all that exists is also to realize that a human person has to help others experience God's

---

27. Migliore, *Faith Seeking Understanding*, 70.

goodness. In short, all people have a responsibility to build the kingdom of God on earth.

The Trinity and the African Understanding of Community

The community constitutes the nature of human living in an African context. There is no human being who is not a member of a community. On the one hand, the reality of community is the basis of human living in Africa that provides a basis for understanding God as the Trinity of persons. On the other hand, the Trinity provides a foundation for understanding the importance of community living among human beings. The fact that God is a community of persons (the Father, the Son, and the Holy Spirit) shows the necessity of communal life. One can say that the personal nature of human beings is realized in the human community and further that the personal nature of God in a way points to the human personal nature created in God's image. Personality is a higher way of being. The fullness of personality can be argued to exist in God, and for this reason human personality can be said to exist as a participation in God's being. The relation between human personality and the personal nature of God can be understood in the way St. Thomas Aquinas perceived the natural law as the way in which human reason participates in the divine eternal reason.[28]

Community presupposes unity. Human community is a way in which human beings come to know the need for unity with one another and with the natural world. In a way, community points to the relatedness of human existence, and the attempt to understand this unity leads to the presupposition of the deity from whom all gain their existence.

The African understanding of community provides a way of talking about God. Human communion in an African context points to something beyond the physical and visible human community. The community has an indescribable spiritual aspect. To know that one belongs to a community is to acknowledge a spiritual bond that joins people together. People may try to explain the reasons for the reality of human community, but there is no simple reason. The existence of a community of persons cannot be simply explained by the concerns of survival or self-preservation. The community, like human nature, goes into the description of what it means to be a human person. Just as one cannot describe a human person

---

28. See Aquinas, *Summa Theologiae*, I–II, qq. 90–97, and especially q. 91, a. 2.

as separate from human nature, so also one cannot describe a community separate from human beings. Could there be a community of animals? The community presupposes human beings, and human beings point to the existence of a community.

The argument can be taken further to imply that the human community points to the possibility of the existence of God. Human community can be viewed as pointing to the relatedness of all of existence. The Christian understanding of God as a community of persons helps understand the spiritual nature of human community. Understanding human community in the perspective of the Trinitarian communion shows the sacredness of the community. From a Christian perspective, the human community points to something beyond itself: it points to God. Hence, the gospel states: "For where two or three are gathered together in my name, there I am in the midst of them" (Matt 18:20).

Christian Life as Life in the Spirit

Christian faith holds God's presence in the world as one of its central tenets. God is believed to be present in the world and among human beings through his Spirit. Hence, Christian life is held to be a life guided by the Spirit of God. The Spirit of God refers to the person of God. To be guided by the Spirit of God is to be guided by God himself. Jesus promised the Spirit to his followers (Luke 24:49). St Paul distinguished between the works of the Spirit and the works of the flesh (Gal 5:16–26). The work of the Spirit of God is the work of creation and providence. The Spirit of God was active in the creation of the heavens and the earth (Gen 1 and 2). The Spirit of God provided for the well-being of the Israelites on their sojourn to the promised land. God was present in the cloud: "Whenever the cloud rose from the Dwelling, the Israelites would set out on their journey" (Exod 40:36).

The gifts of the Spirit are referred to as wisdom, understanding, counsel, knowledge, strength, the fear of the Lord, justice, and faithfulness (Isa 11:1–5). To be a person of faith is to be open to the guidance of the Spirit of God. Christian spiritual life is thought of as a life in the Spirit of God. Guided by the Spirit of God, Christians understand themselves to possess a responsibility to help build the kingdom of God on earth. To be a person of faith is to take upon oneself the divine life given by the grace of God.

The Social Nature of the Christian Faith

The understanding of the Christian life as the life in the Spirit is the foundation to the understanding of the Christian contribution to help bring about the good life in society. The Christian is moved by God's Spirit to help bring about justice on earth. Christian life is not just a way of being; it is also a way of life. It is a way of practical living guided by love. St. Paul exhorted the Christian communities:

> I, then, a prisoner for the Lord, urge you to live in a manner worthy of the call you have received, with all humility and gentleness, with patience, bearing with one another through love, striving to preserve the unity of the spirit through the bond of peace: one body and one Spirit, as you were also called to the one hope of your call; one Lord, one faith, one baptism; one God and Father of all, who is over all and through all and in all. (Eph 4:1-8)

The life and ministry of Jesus Christ is the best example of witness of life to those who have faith in him. The Christian gospels in the New Testament are the best source of understanding the Christian life. Jesus in the gospels is not only said to have told the people of his time about the Kingdom of God, but he also raised issues that affected their earthly well being. Hence, the golden rule: "Do to others whatever you would have them do to you. This is the law and the prophets" (Matt 7:12). He fed the hungry and cured the sick (Matt 4:23-25) and also called people to love their neighbors as themselves (Luke 10:27). The commandment of love was presented by Jesus as the summary of his teachings and that of the Hebrew Scriptures (Luke 10:25-28). In the teachings of Jesus, love is to be extended not only to one's friends but also to one's enemies (Matt 5:43-44, cf. Luke 6:27-28). Most of all, Jesus could claim to have the Spirit of God: "The Spirit of the Lord is upon me, because he has anointed me to bring glad tidings to the poor. He has sent me to proclaim liberty to captives and recovery of sight to the blind, to let the oppressed go free, and to proclaim a year acceptable to the Lord" (Luke 4:18-19). Hence, just as it was in the mission of Jesus Christ to bring about good news to the poor, that is, help them overcome their physical, spiritual, and social ills, so also it is for the Christian community. The praxis of Jesus is supposed to be the core of the praxis and being of the Christian community.

PART THREE

The Praxis of the Christian Faith

Having noted that praxis as taught by liberation theology has the risk of becoming a theory like any abstract theological method, I wish to suggest some ways that the redeeming nature of Christianity can be brought about to impact social transformation.

Christian faith and teachings are inseparable from Christian action. Christians as people living in the world have an indispensable role of promoting the quality of life in their respective societies. However, as noted before, history is filled with the problem of separating Christian life from societal life.

A sound Christian theology understands the world and its inhabitants as willed by God, and therefore, it has an inherent obligation to promote human life and its natural environment. The preceding is a basis for an ethics that views promotion of life forms as constituting good morals and whatever diminishes life forms as immoral. Praxis as the transforming action in any society should move Christians to work for good governance as well as helping realize a just society where no one is excluded from sharing in the common good.

There are many ways a Christian can get involved in advocating for social transformation. For example, some people write letters to their representatives in government to raise their concerns on a particular issue. In extreme cases, civil disobedience can be a way of bringing about the desired transformation. But of great significance is the power of the ballot through democratic election of a good government. In addition, the ways of bringing about social transformation differ in any given society and also in different historical epochs. For example, over the last decade public demonstrations and protests have effected change in some African countries.

It can also be contended that any good change in a society requires some commensurate actions. One person cannot perform a job that can only be done by over a hundred people. Good social change requires the participation of as many people as possible. Just as different tools are required to accomplish different tasks, so also should Christians bring about their variety of gifts in the work for the beneficial transformation of society (1 Cor 13). However, it is imperative to keep in mind that political problems require in most cases inclusive political actions and solutions. Applied in an African context, there is a need for people who can make the "necessary noise" and action to promote adherence to the rule of law. People who can stand up to the powers that be to bring about equity and justice are an undeniable asset for the well being of any society. Case in point is the National Council of Churches and National Catholic Conference of Bishops in some African countries who have been a voice of the people for quite some time now through open letters and press releases. Another example is the writing of a new constitution in Kenya that was meant to ensure good governance and was brought about by Christians and other people who were essentially moved by their faith to action.

To bring about just social change in any society requires all the facets that define a human being in an integral way. These human dimensions that are required, especially in the elimination of the evil of poverty and its accompanying suffering, include religious, spiritual, psychological, social, political, and economic solutions. In a complementary way, other sciences, such as the social and the natural sciences, would serve theology well in finding relevant ways to tackle social problems. To eradicate poverty, there is a need to go to the root cause of it. An example is the Catholic Diocese of Murang'a in Kenya where besides raising questions on corruption in government, the church, through the diocesan development offices, has been concerned with initiating projects such as providing running water, agricultural services, medical care, and other services for the sole purpose of aiding the people in need. Civics education is also carried out to make people aware of their rights and what can be done to ensure those rights.

Praxis as a Pastoral Concern: Christian Community as a Center of Transforming Action

The pastoral ministry of a Christian church is to proclaim the salvation brought about by Jesus Christ. This proclamation usually consists of the presentation of the word of God and the social action flowing from the hearers and believers of the word. The task of all people involved in the pastoral ministry, having understood the kingdom of God as proclaimed by Jesus as including all people, is therefore one of bringing about the transformation of the whole society. It is the humanization of all people— ensuring that all people realize the dignity of the image of God given them at creation. The sacramental life of the Church has a social dimension, since all people are invited to share in God's grace. A sacrament is a symbol of God's presence on earth as witnessed in the life of a believer.

Christian faith is addressed to the individual human person in a community. The conversion to faith implies the transformation of the individual that is envisaged in the context of the Christian community. It is taking upon oneself the way of Christ. It is to become a new creation, a new being in Christ, and being a member of the body of Christ, the Church (Eph 5:29–30). Individual conversion has implications also to the wider community. Good individuals are the catalysts and agents of improving life in the community.

The Christian community is a symbol or sacrament of God's love. It is an assembly of the people who know they are loved by the compassionate God, and they in turn share that love with one another. As the salt and light of the world, the Christian community understands that its mission is to illumine the wider society with love and hope.[29] It is the city built on a hilltop or a lit lamp placed on a stand that should not be hidden under a bushel basket (Matt 5:13–16). Christians view themselves as having a responsibility to witness to hope and trust in God. This is especially evident in small rural areas in Africa where the life of a Christian community is seen outside the church in everyday living in ways such as helping the sick and the needy. Early Christian community was recognizable through the love shared by all in the community (1 John 4:13–21).

The Christian calling is an invitation to participate in the mission and the self-giving life of Jesus Christ. Jesus Christ preached the kingdom of God and suffered and died to free humanity from sin. Christ is believed to continually work as liberator in and through the Christian community. The historical mission of Christ had some practical aspects in it: repentance and believing that the kingdom of God has come in the person of Jesus Christ (Mark 1:15). The problem would be to "spiritualize" or "mystify" what should otherwise be simple, practical action effecting radical, positive change. Radical change consists of true conversion from sin and has social implications. It is also addressing real problems affecting real people that require concrete and actual response. The Epistle of St. James

---

29. See what Moltmann states: "The hope that is staked on the creator *ex nihilo* becomes the happiness of the present when it loyally embraces all things in love, abandoning nothing to annihilation but bringing to light how open all things are to the possibilities in which they can live and shall live" (*Theology of Hope*, 32).

has emphatically taught that telling the poor "to keep warm and one will pray for them" does not keep them warm and well fed (James 2:15–17).

In a concrete way, the Christian community has the power to transform the larger society, especially through advocacy work. The work of the churches is seen through the implementation of education and social programs. Justice and peace commissions in the Catholic Church are one way this church in some places has tried to bring about human development and a just society. Justice and peace are inseparable because you cannot have peace without justice; one points to the other.

The Sacramental Nature of Christian Living (Praxis)

Christian praxis is to be understood in a sacramental way. Sacraments are instruments of God's grace in the practice of the Christian religion. In a sacrament are material and physical signs, such as water in the sacrament of baptism or bread and wine in the sacrament of the Eucharist. Besides the visible and material signs, sacraments have a form that is the performance of the ritual, such as the words used while pouring water in the sacrament of baptism. For example, while pouring water during the celebration of the sacrament of baptism, a priest says: "John Noteworthy, I baptize you in the name of God the Father, the Son, and the Holy Spirit." Since Christian living particularly is a life of grace, there is no Christianity without the sacraments. Sacraments are symbolic manifestations of the grace of God. God gives himself to all of creation, and therefore we can say that to live is to be open to God's grace. Sacraments have a social nature. Besides being understood as instituted by Jesus Christ and left to the stewardship of the church, sacraments are also viewed as effecting an intimate relationship among human beings and God. The sacraments are also believed to provide an opportunity for Christians to realize that the world is the work of God and all people are the children of God.

For example, the social action in a Catholic parish is nourished by the celebration of the word of God and the sacraments. In baptism, all the people are called to new life, and in confirmation believers are given the gift of the spirit to witness to God's love. The Eucharist nourishes people in their daily struggles to minister to one another in love. At the end of the celebration of the Eucharist the congregation is sent away to serve God through loving and serving one another.[30] In an African context, the new

---

30. See the Order of the Mass in *The Sacramentary*, 567.

life of faith symbolized by the sacrament of baptism is the beginning of the baptized person's mission in the community. Baptism has not only an individual character of grace to the one being baptized but also incorporates one as a member of the community of faith. This membership calls for a responsible life of justice and love. The baptized person becomes an agent of Christ's love to all. The sacraments of baptism and confirmation confer the Spirit of the new life in Christ. The three sacraments (baptism, confirmation, and Eucharist) are referred to as the sacraments of Christian initiation. They make a person a member of Christ's body, the Church.

The sacraments of baptism, confirmation, and Eucharist give the Spirit of the new life in Christ. This new life calls for the initiates to shape their life in the way of Christ. The self-giving love of Christ in his life, ministry, passion, and death embodies the vocation of the Christian faithful. An African understanding of the sacraments can lead to a person's appreciation of the significance of not only the celebration of the sacrament but also the living of the sacramental life. Some African theologians have suggested African traditional rites of passage as proper ways of understanding the significance of the sacraments in an African context.[31] An African person's life is marked by different stages celebrated through rituals such as birth, circumcision, marriage, and becoming a member of the council of elders, etc. The sacraments, like African rites of passage, mark the process of maturation of the initiates in the Christian faith and the incorporation into the Christian community.

The sacrament of the Eucharist is the celebration of the sacrifice of Christ on the cross and the entire paschal mystery of Christ: passion, crucifixion, death, and resurrection. The sacrifice of Jesus Christ is the model of love where the Son of God died for the world. To emulate the action of Christ is to be ready to share one's life with other people—for example, doing something to change or improve situations of suffering to ones of love and hope. The Eucharist as a sacrament of the self-giving love of Christ is a foundation for Christians to give themselves for the good of others. It is the sacrament that embodies Christ's service to his disciples and all of humanity. Like Jesus, Christian believers in the sacrament of the Eucharist are called to "wash one another's feet." John 13:12–15 states:

> So when he had washed their feet [and] put his garments back on and reclined at table again, he said to them, "Do you realize what I

---

31. Magesa, *African Religion*, 97.

have done for you? You call me 'teacher' and 'master,' and rightly so, for indeed I am. If I, therefore, the master and teacher, have washed your feet, you ought to wash one another's feet. I have given you a model to follow, so that as I have done for you, you should also do."

Hence, the sacrament of the Eucharist is understood as the celebration of the memorial of Christ's action of offering his life for the salvation of all. Those who participate in the Eucharistic celebration are reminded to participate in Christ's action by offering themselves for the well-being of their fellow human beings and all of creation in the universe.

In the sacrament of reconciliation, the believer is called to accept the forgiving love of Christ by forgiving oneself and others. The sacrament of reconciliation acknowledges the alienation that is effected by sin. Sin destroys the community while reconciliation builds and mends the brokenness in the community. The traditional African society clearly understood the social nature of sin. The sin of one person was seen to have far-reaching consequences to the whole community. For example, an individual sin was thought to cause drought, famine, and disease. The social nature of sin is evident in modern Africa, especially in corruption of some public officials who embezzle public funds.

Reconciliation can help overcome divisions. In human society, there are ambiguities of divisions based on tribe, race, age, and religion, among others. Contemporary Africa has experienced various genocides caused by religious differences, tribalism, and political affiliation. The Rwanda genocide of 1994 comes to mind or even the Darfur crisis in Sudan where thousands have been killed because of their ethnicity.

Reconciliation also can be brought to solve the various civil wars in Africa. In the Democratic Republic of Congo, natural resources such as diamonds as well as tribalism and regionalism have been the bases of the civil war that has killed and displaced thousands of people. Nigeria has been a melting pot of religious conflicts between the Muslims and the Christians. Headline news is announced from time to time about the killing of hundreds of people in a day of religious conflict in northern Nigeria. In all these conflicts, the spilling of human blood can be stopped if the people come together. The Christian community should be an example of forgiveness and reconciliation and through this, reaching out to people of other religious faiths.

Generally, the sacraments are about the liberating or redeeming love of God. They are meant to spur the Christian faithful to social action as well as spiritual growth. The liberation life of the Christian parish is nourished by the word of God and the sacraments. Parochial liturgy is a celebration of God's saving work and invitation of all people to be "co-saviors" with God and Jesus Christ. It is a life of helping to build the kingdom of God on earth. The kingdom of God is supposed to be viewed as encompassing the integral well-being of God's people and the world. It has religious, socio-political, and economic implications.

Liberation is action that brings about change in society.[32] It is the overcoming of all alienation brought about by systemic and personal structures of sin and also the proclamation of the kingdom of God, a kingdom of justice and peace. It is the empowerment of the people. True liberation should promote social change brought about by the people themselves who are affected and dehumanized by situations of oppression, poverty, and disease. However, others outside the affected society should also be in solidarity by helping, where possible, the dehumanized people achieve the empowerment that restores their dignity and brings about social transformation. Liberation should foster the self-determination of a people, thus affirming the people's capacity to know and bring about what is needed for their integral well being. The parish, especially in Africa, should be the center from which liberation is ignited.

Further, liberation also has to be understood as solidarity with those in any form of need.[33] It is bringing into mainstream the people who have been relegated to the margins of society. There is a required awareness that the poor as human beings are people who can also effect social change. Any outside help should be conceived of as facilitating this change beginning from within the Christian community. The work of liberation extends from the grassroots to encompass a whole nation.

The National Episcopal Conferences and the Council of Churches and Other Religions

From the above, the role of Christian churches to work for positive societal change both at the national level and the grassroots communities is evident. One way of bringing about this social change is through the

---

32. Miller and Grenz, *Fortress Introduction to Contemporary Theologies*, 142–58.
33. Mieth, "Solidarity and the Right to Work," 58.

The Social Nature of the Christian Faith

National Council of Churches and Episcopal Conferences in various African countries and also other national groups such as the Christian Women's Association and the Association of Religious Women and Men. Roman Catholic bishops in a particular country usually organize themselves into a national conference that is a representative body of the various dioceses. On their part, the Protestant churches have a national council of churches, among other groups, that do very effective social advocacy work.[34] Catholic national conferences of bishops are also an effective tool for raising important social issues. For example, the Kenya Episcopal Conference has been known to voice concerns with the government on social-political issues in the country. Laurenti Magesa evaluates the work of Tanzanian Roman Catholic National Episcopal Conference as follows:

> The third message of 1993 bore the title *Clear Conscience: The Direction of Our Nation*. The aim of the message was to help people recognize the political situation in the country and to examine the problems and causes facing the nation. How can citizens recognize, protect, and defend their rights?[35]

Further, Magesa states:

> *Some Guidelines from the Catholics Bishops of Tanzania for the National Elections of October 1995* was issued in 1994 in both English and Swahili. It reiterated the basic principles upon which the nation was built: human dignity, justice, peace, equality, freedom, respect for all, unity, wisdom, patriotism, self-confidence, and self-reliance. The letter then elaborated each of those principles in the context of a multiparty democracy.[36]

While it is good that Protestant churches have national councils and Roman Catholic dioceses have a united front through national conferences of bishops, among other associations, ecumenism and Christian unity is a major way people of different religions, and even various Christian denominations, can come together to work to bring about social and political transformation in a society. This is possible in many places in Africa because religion is a major influence in people's lives. Peter Katjavivi states the following on the history of Namibia's fight against apartheid and for political independence:

34. See *The National Council of Churches of Kenya*.
35. Magesa, *Anatomy of Inculturation*, 186.
36. Ibid., 187.

The transformation of the churches to the point where they were prepared to face national issues and stand against the colonial authorities was slow. But when it came it brought with it a formidable strength of opposition to South African rule. After 1971 the churches forged a unity between themselves and with other social forces which greatly strengthened the political struggle. The ecumenical Christian Centre in Windhoek, founded in the mid-1970s, provided an educational and cultural centre and a forum for the exchange of ideas and debate about the nature and direction of the struggle for independence. In 1977, the Council of Churches of Namibia (CCN) was formed and provided further opportunities for the various church denominations to come together to share their experience and make joint statements on matters of common interest. The CCN is an ecumenical body whose concerns extend from religious to social and educational matters. It was originally made up of the following churches: African Methodist Episcopal Church (AME); Anglican Diocese of Namibia; Evangelical Lutheran Church in Namibia (ELCIN); Methodist Church; and Roman Catholic Church (RCC). The Dutch Reformed Church has never been part of the CCN. The German Evangelical Lutheran Church became observers, and then members, but withdrew from the CCN in 1987, accusing it of being too politicised.[37]

The conferences of bishops and the ecumenical and interdenominational councils of churches are major ways the people of various religious backgrounds can address the various issues affecting their respective societies. Issues affecting people of different faiths, when considered from their human perspective, become a uniting force and thereby a force for effecting social transformation. For example, Christian churches can work together with members of the Islamic faith and other world religions to foster human development such as providing healthcare and other essential services for human living.

Conclusion

This chapter detailed various ways the social nature of Christianity is brought to bear in making human living better. The praxis of Christian teachings and pastoral praxis is seen as an effective way to bring about positive social transformation at a grassroots level. From the local parish to the conference of bishops or national council of churches, Christianity is viewed as inherently a social faith. The next chapter deals with various

37. Katjavivi, "The Role of the Church in the Struggle for Independence," 14–15.

ways the social nature of the Christian religion is realized in a historical setting and the theological methods that show its relevance.

3

Method in African Theology

To study theology is to reflect on the reality of the world, human beings, and God. As mentioned before in this work, theology is concerned with a people's response to the events of their lives as well as a search aimed at understanding the meaning of their lives, their beginnings, their goals, and their ends. To engage in the theological study of the reality of human existence, the world, and God, there is need for a systematic process. This systematization of thought is what is otherwise referred to as a method. A method provides a systematic way for people to process their thoughts or even to show how they have reached the positions they hold. Engagement with reality in a reflective way leads to recognition of the necessity of a method.

The need for a theological method is irreplaceable in any theological inquiry, especially in an African context. African theology began to gain momentum from the 1960s onward. The theological methods of inculturation and liberation have dominated most of the works that have been published in African theology. However, the task of analyzing African theology is not that simple, since there are as many theological methods as there are theologians. In this work I argue that African theologies are not limited to any one theological methodology. There are not only varieties of methods in African theology but also the need for openness to theological methods from other parts of the world. For example, without denying that the concept of liberation is not foreign to Africa, it is undeniable that African theology is influenced by the liberation theological method from Latin America, which in turn is somehow influenced by the European political theology. The inculturation method in African theology relates to the historical and cultural consciousness, especially in the mid to late twentieth century. Although African theology can be

Method in African Theology

categorized as distinct in its use of African history, it will be seen to have been open to influence by theologies from elsewhere in the world.

It is important to emphasize here that methodologically African theology is not independent of other theologies in the world. It shares in methodology with other theologies in the world, such as the existential and anthropological approach. For example, many African theologians approach theology from an African historical context, emphasizing issues such as colonialism and post-colonialism, while others give a more prominent place to the traditional religions of Africa. What difference, if any, is there between African theological methods and theological methods in other parts of the world? In terms of method, different theologians share some aspects such as a historical awareness in their analyses and researches. Any theological method could have gaps that other approaches can help fill. Hence, one can argue that theological methods are complementary, and openness to various theological approaches highlights the nature of theological study.

Nevertheless, in African theology, there is a need for theological methods that are genuinely African and drawn from an African context. From the above, any theological method can be referred to as trans-cultural, that is, shared by various cultures. The point to remain aware of is that African theology is also influenced by theological developments in other parts of the world. From its own unique perspective, African theology has a task to develop its genuinely African methods.

The central argument in this work is that no single method is adequate enough in the study of theology. There are many theological methods: historical, transcendental or existential, liberation, inculturation, process, and feminist, among others. However, the distinction between the various methods is sometimes one of emphases rather than irreconcilable differences. For example, an existential theology like that of Karl Rahner and the political theology such as that of Johann Metz are distinct from each other solely in their approach on history. While Rahner emphasizes the human person as the subject who has a capacity for rational knowledge and knowledge of God, Metz shows that the human person is shaped by historical and social factors, and further, according to Metz, theology has to concern itself with historical events that affect human living.[1]

---

1. Moltmann has also argued for the Christian role in history. See *Creating a Just Future*, 24–29.

Historical and Social Dimensions in African Christian Theology

With an understanding of the relationship and limitations in theological methods, anybody who ventures into the study of theology should be willing and open to explore the various points of view as realized through various theological methodologies. Due to the need for interaction in theological methods, this section evaluates the various theological methods that have taken shape in contemporary theology and interconnects them by showing their relationship by even suggesting how one method relates to and differs from another. The suggestion here is that inculturation as a method in theology can be taken as a vantage point to evaluate other theological methods. To be meaningful, all theology has to be open to culture and hence all theology can be referred to as a process of inculturation. The second part of this chapter presents the emergence of Small Christian Communities (SCCs) in Africa as a tool for evaluating the relevance of various theological methods.

PART ONE

Inculturation as a Method and a Theology

One of the main goals of African theology can be referred to as inculturation. Inculturation is both a theological method as well as the goal of theological study. Its aim is to bring about an understanding of the Christian faith in a cultural-historical context. The inculturation method is the process that involves engaging a particular culture with the Christian gospel. Inculturation runs through the work of many African theologians. It is what appears to tie African theology together. The question of method in African theology is not a simple one. But even with the enormous size and diversity of the African continent, African theologians address the same or related issues from different methodological perspectives.

Inculturation is notably the dominant theological method in African theology. According to Robert Schreiter:

> Inculturation, as a noun, is often used . . . in theological process as well. A combination of the theological principle of incarnation with the social-science concept of acculturation (adapting oneself to a culture), the term has come to be used widely in Roman Catholic circles and appears in many documents of congresses and episcopal conferences. It refers to the wider process of which theology is an expression.[2]

---

2. Schreiter, *Constructing Local Theologies*, 5.

Inculturation is concretely the main issue on which African theology hangs. However, there is also diversity in how the inculturation method is used. One could say the issue of African identity is crucial in African theology, and inculturation theologies attempt to define and enhance a genuine African understanding of humanity, God, and the African worldview. In African theology one can see a development in analysis of what it means to be an African human being. Schreiter distinguishes inculturation from adaptation. He refers to the work of Placide Tempel, *Bantu Philosophy*, as adaptation. Tempel used a Neo-Thomistic philosophical framework and redeveloped it with equivalent categories from the Bantu people in the Belgian Congo.[3] "The early work of the Tanzanian theologian Charles Nyamiti is an example of this (adaptation model). He called for the use of local materials to construct a philosophical system parallel to the Neo-Thomist ones he had learned at the University of Louvain."[4]

On adaptation model, Schreiter analyzes its strengths thus:

> Especially when wielded in the hands of local leaders, it can quickly help to achieve the twin goals of some authenticity in the local culture and respectability in Western church circles. The theology that emerges from such a model is replete with the categories, names, and concerns of a local culture, yet looks like Western theology and is relatively easily understood by Westerners. Moreover, it makes dialogue between North Atlantic and other churches much easier, since fundamentally similar frameworks are in use. It can give younger churches a sense of equal status with the older, more established churches.[5]

Although dialogue with the rest of the universal church is important, the main focus should be the local people's understanding and practice of their faith. From Schreiter's point of view, the main concern should be showing the role of the local communities in theological processes. Later in this work, I have suggested the Small Christian Communities as a basis for evaluating the strengths and weaknesses of theological methods. The main concern of the local theology is the local people and their context. Schreiter states:

---

3. Ibid., 9.
4. Ibid., 10.
5. Ibid.

The contextual models, as the name implies, concentrate more directly on the cultural context in which Christianity takes root and receives expression. Whereas the adaptation models continue to emphasize somewhat more the received faith, contextual models begin their reflection with the cultural context. Contextual models are seen increasingly as embodying the ideals of what local theology is to be about, even though the working out of those ideals often proves difficult in the practice.[6]

Furthermore, there is weakness in the adaptation theological model because it ". . . presumes a method in theology whereby an articulated philosophical foundation forms the basis for a systematic theology."[7] However, adaptation is better than translation approach.

Below I suggest various ways to understand the process of inculturation of the Christian faith. These suggestions are: inculturation as dialogue, inculturation as correlation, and inculturation as what happens in the Small Christian Communities (SCCs) in contemporary Africa.

Inculturation as Dialogue

Dialogue is a way of achieving inculturation and can also be referred to as what constitutes inculturation. In an African setting, besides all the other methods that have gained prominence in theological studies, I find dialogue as a more relevant way to understand the process of inculturation. Although dialogue is not emphasized enough in African theology, it seems to be the essence of theological discourse that is genuinely inter-cultural. Dialogue assumes an attitude of openness. However, the question remains of who the dialogue partners are. Besides the theologian, the dialogue partners are mainly the Christian believers and those on the way to faith and can also include members of other world religions. The theologian, as a member of a community who participates in the dialogue, but also as a professional, has a capacity to analyze the community's dialogue with the Christian teachings. Theological dialogue should be concerned with concrete issues that affect human living and the human relationship with God.

It is not enough to study theology in school, for it requires a reflection in the life of a community, and it is for this reason that African

6. Ibid., 12.
7. Ibid., 10.

Method in African Theology

inculturation theology has found deep roots in the Christian communities in the continent. There may not be so much mention of theological methods as such, but the basic aspect in the process of inculturation is an application of the Christian teachings into the life of a people. It is what Nyamiti refers to as inculturation Christologies done in a way of comparative analogy. It is the intrinsic employment of African cultural themes in order that people may have an understanding of the Christian mysteries. This process consists of an identification of the African element with the Christian mystery and the explication of the implications underlying such identification.[8] This calls for dialogue, which Nyamiti sees to have metaphysical problems and questions, and interestingly, he sees African theology to be under the tutelage of St. Thomas Aquinas.[9]

The Christian faithful are the ones who dialogue with their faith as presented in the sacred Scriptures and the sacred tradition, and theology studies this interaction. This dialogue is what constitutes theological study and inculturation. The theologian is a participant in the dialogue of faith as well as one who can facilitate it. Through dialogue with the universal church, Africa develops her own tradition. An African Christian tradition should not be seen to go against the unity of the Church but on the contrary, it should be viewed as strengthening the unity of the universal Church. However, some Christian denominations have been critical of African expressions in the celebration of the liturgy.

Further, dialogue is a way of building the community of faith. Through dialogue, all people involved become active participants in the life of the community. And without dialogue, people can be passive and possibly disengaged with community life. The pastoral and parish councils, advocated by the Second Vatican Council and the 1983 Code of Canon Law,[10] are an effective way to promote dialogue in the Christian community.

Dialogue in the Church would ensure that people participate in understanding and developing doctrines and ritual practices and this way make them their own. Church teachings should be an outcome of the process of dialogue between the Christian faithful, their own pastors, and

---

8. Nyamiti, "Contemporary African Christologies," 68–69.

9. Ibid., 70–72.

10. The *Code of Canon Law*, no. 512 paragraph 1 states: "A pastoral council is composed of members of Christ's faithful who are in full communion with the Catholic Church: clerics, members of institutes of consecrated life, and especially lay people."

those in leadership positions in the churches. This dialogue process would ensure that teachings in the church are not dictations from the clergy and hierarchy but that they emanate from the whole church as the body of Christ. However, within the various Christian doctrines, such as on faith, morals, and ritual, people can creatively structure their life within their worldview.

Since people change with time, dialogue is supposed to always be a continuous process. Creative dialogue with the Christian faith does not encourage complacency but understands the dynamic nature of a people's thought and language over time. A community of faith that dialogues would therefore be a community that grows and develops. It is centered on the people and their faith in God. This constitutes the spirit of true theology—that is, a theology based on daily interaction with the believers' faith in God and their world (culture), as opposed to a theology to be found in textbooks only.

The inculturation model of theology comprises of an intellectual and spiritual dialogue with the faith. The purpose of dialogue between people is to bring about understanding. However, dialogue can be referred to as inculturation because to understand another person or teaching, one uses one's cultural elements such as language and symbols. Any member of a Christian community is supposed to be a participant, a dialogue partner with other community members and consequently with people outside the immediate community. Inculturation is not to be viewed as a preserve of the professional theologian but the responsibility of every Christian faithful who wants to understand the faith. Dialogue is not reserved for the experts but for people who engage themselves with the simple tasks of their daily life and their faith. Consequently, inculturation is to be understood as dialogue. True inculturation has to be conceived of as people dialoguing with one another and their faith. Later dialogue will be seen as the main feature in the Small Christian Communities in many parts of Africa.

Dialogue in an African setting facilitates the possibility for openness to other theological traditions. The aim of dialogue, or communication, for that matter, is to promote harmony and understanding. Dialogue can be used as a theological method that brings convergence of all theological methods and thought systems. Since dialogue is not sectarian but is open to other views and cultures, it can be said to be an enriching process where people encounter one another and bring in wealth of experiences and practices.[11]

In a fundamental way, theology is shaped by the community of the theologian. An inculturation theologian is one who helps sustain the dialogue between the community and academia. She or he is aware of what is going on in the community of faith and also has time to analyze that community experience in her or his study and research. The effectiveness of a theological system can be known by its faithfulness to the community and ultimately its meaningfulness in the community as a whole. In the Christian community, whether in a diocese or parish, dialogue would help realize the communion of faith. This in turn would lead to a wholly mature and integrated Christian life.

In a concrete setting, dialogue is what builds a community of faith, and since dialogue is shaped by a people's cultural and linguistic background, there cannot be dialogue without inculturation, and there is no inculturation without dialogue.

Inculturation as a Correlation between Faith and Culture

To understand something, people relate or associate it with some previous experience. People correlate their experiences in daily living. The theological method of correlation takes a cultural element and relates it with some teaching in the Bible or in the church doctrine. This is especially evident among African theologians who take a particular teaching in the Bible and show how it is similar to an African traditional belief and practice.

Paul Tillich is an example of a theologian who extensively developed the method of correlation in the study of Christian theology. He viewed theology as concerned with human questions about God. Theology tries to understand the human situation, and according to Tillich, the human

---

11. See what B. Bujo wrote about palaver in African ethics: "Palaver is by no means superfluous talk or useless negotiation but an efficient institutionalization of communicative action. If an important decision is to be arrived at over matters that affect the people as a community, the wisest representatives of the people are called together for a palaver.... In the palaver, the only thing that counts is competence and experience. They are the ones who share daily life with the people, so that their argumentation is concerned with the people's existential interests, often to the smallest detail. In order to find a solution for a problem, they share their experiences, refer to the entire history of the clan community, and consider the interests of both the living and the dead" (*The Ethical Dimension of Community*, 36).

situation requires courage. Courage implies hope in the search for understanding of the human being and the world. He describes courage as an affirmation of one's being as well as an ethical act.[12] From Tillich's perspective, experience is the medium through which the sources of theology speak to us. However, he carefully argues that experience receives and does not produce theology.[13] James Livingston sums Tillich's work as follows:

> In his Systematic Theology Tillich undertakes this mediating task by exhibiting a correlation between religion and culture. The relation between the two, he suggests, is like the correlation between "questioning" and "answering" in a conversation. Or, it is like the correlation between "form" and "content" (or "substance") in a work of art. Indeed, it is possible to correlate them because in concrete reality "religion" and "culture" are always a single whole of which "the form of religion is culture and the substance of culture is religion."[14]

Tillich suggests that the human condition always raises fundamental questions that human cultures express in various ways in the dominant styles of their work of art and to which religious traditions offer answers expressed in religious symbols. Accordingly, he organizes his "Systematic Theology" in five parts. In each part a major biblical religious symbol is correlated as an "answer" to a major human question as expressed by modern culture.[15] Tillich draws from Kierkegaard and Nietzsche the idea that the experience of our lives is on the edge of being overwhelmed by meaninglessness, guilt, and death. "Being" is threatened by "non-being." But the "answer" is provided by the Christian symbol of "God as Creator."[16] Tillich's explanation of who Jesus is follows from explanation of what he did to "save" us.[17]

Some of what has been happening in the development of African theology can be referred to as correlation in its approach. There is in African theology an undertaking of dialogue between African traditional culture and the biblical and western Christian tradition. Besides tradi-

---

12. Tillich, *Courage to Be*, 2–3.
13. Ibid., 3.
14. Livingston, *Modern Christian Thought*, 136.
15. Ibid., 136–37.
16. Ibid.
17. Ibid., 143.

Method in African Theology

tional cultures, many African people correlate the Bible with their current situation in life. Itumeleng Mosala states the following on African Independent Churches in South Africa:

> Many other black working class people in non-sub-cultural religious contexts appropriate the Bible in terms of its contents. Many *Madodana* (men's guilds) or *Manyano* (women's guilds), while not having significantly more education, have been assimilated into a reading culture of the Bible. Thus for them the authority of the Bible derives from its contents. Consequently a specifically black working class hermeneutics, drawing its weapons largely from the work place experiences, is discernible in these groups. This hermeneutics addresses the contradiction of class relatively less ideologically. As such it represents a better chance of enabling its bearers to find a resolution to the problematic of the entire class of which they are members.[18]

Mosala distinguishes between the reading of the Bible among people with no religious affiliation and the reading by people affiliated to a religious denomination. He states:

> It is not so with the sub-cultural members of the AICs [African Independent Churches] who form a part of this same class. Theirs is a more symbolically pitched attempt to resolve the problem. While it does enable them to negotiate their reality and even to resist the forces of brutalisation with which the whole class is faced, their hermeneutical weapons are not drawn from the concrete experiences of the work place and social life of its members. Instead, they are derived from the mystifications generated by the authoritative status of an unread Bible (brackets mine).[19]

A people's experience is brought to bear upon their reading of a text, including the Bible. Most importantly, the reading of the Bible can help the believer understand how God intervenes in his or her pain and hopelessness, and consequently how to bring about peace and justice in the working and living conditions of the readers.

In the inculturation method there is a correlation of the Christian faith to the local culture of its adherents. The inculturation method, as well as the correlation method, is concerned with developing an understanding of the Christian message in a culturally relevant way. The

---

18. Mosala, "Race, Class, and Gender as Hermeneutical Factors," 55.
19. Ibid.

correlation method seeks answers in the Bible to existential concerns of human living in society. Inculturation promotes a dialogue between the Christian faith and the cultural setting of the faithful. Like correlation, inculturation seeks a way to express the faith and issues of human living in a culturally relevant way.

Below, I propose that the recent development of the Small Christian Communities in African Christian parishes provides a forum for testing the viability of a theological method in its application in a concrete historical context.

PART TWO

Small Christian Communities (SCCs) and Theological Analysis in an African Context

The Small Christian Communities (SCCs) are viewed in this section as the basic means and goal in the process of developing a theology of inculturation. The SCCs are generally understood as the church in the grassroots. They are the best demonstration of the post-Vatican Council II view of the church as the people of God. Both the Roman Catholic Church and Protestant churches in Africa emphasize the importance of SCCs in the daily life of the believers. A suggestion is made here that the strength of theological methods can be tested by their appropriateness in the life of the SCCs. The SCCs in both the Roman Catholic Church and Protestant churches in Africa provide a way to assess and evaluate theological developments. However, in this work I focus on the SCCs as understood and practiced in the African Catholic Church.

The section begins with a description of the nature of a Small Christian Community (SCC). The SCCs are understood to have evolved from the teaching ministry of the Roman Catholic Church after the Second Vatican Council. Finally, the section analyzes some theological methods such as liberation, the anthropological approach, and the historical approach in the light of the SCC movement in Africa. The strength of any theological method is seen through its relevance to the life of the SCCs in an African historical context.

What Is a Small Christian Community in an African Context?

When I visited a number of SCCs in Kenya, I listened and observed how people lived and understood their Christian life every day. When

I write about SCCs, I refer to my experience and theological reflection. The *Kiswahili*[20] name for SCC is *Jumuiya ndogo ndogo*, literally translated as the "really very small" community. The more symbolic is the *Gikuyu* language name for the SCC, which is *Mwaki*, which literally means fire and is taken to refer to people sitting together around a fire warming themselves. In a *Mwaki*, the fire is the sharing of the word of God, love and communion between people, and the prayers offered by members of the community to God.

The terms "basic" and "small" in the case of SCC are used interchangeably. An SCC refers to a group of Christians who live in the same village or neighborhood. It is not a parish but a constituent part of the parish. A parish would comprise of several Christian communities. To understand the SCCs, one needs to know about the parish structures in many parts of Africa. Normally, parishes in rural areas would have a number of outstations (or mission churches). The parish priests travel on Sunday to the outstations for the celebration of sacraments. These outstations would in turn have a number of SCCs. An SCC would generally have between fifteen to twenty members. The members generally meet once a week in the home of one of their members. Generally, in the meeting the members sit outside the house in a circle. Usually, an SCC has rotating leadership, who are given titles such as "servant."

In a meeting of the SCC, shared prayers are said aloud, the word of God is read, and people are invited to share their thoughts and reflections based on the Scripture reading. People also discuss the issues that are happening in their community and suggestions are made on how to help anybody they know who could be in any form of need. Visiting the sick is carried out by members of the SCCs as a group. Sometimes, besides prayers and words of encouragement in the Christian life and depending on need, the members of the SCCs help the people in need. The SCCs are also a means for preparing communal events such as weddings, visiting those with newborn babies, baptisms, funerals, etc.

Basically, the life of the parish community revolves around the SCCs. SCCs are not exclusive but mutually inclusive. One SCC participates in the events prepared by another SCC. The parish priests, to be effective in their pastoral ministry, have to always know and participate in the

---

20. Generally many people refer to Swahili as the language while actually it is the name of the Swahili people of the East African coast. Their language is properly known as Kiswahili.

various celebrations in the SCCs. Some priests have felt threatened by SCCs through the mistaken view of SCCs as usurping their "power." However, this misconceived threat is due to a disconnection between the priests and the SCCs. A priest in a parish has to actively engage by visiting the SCCs in his parish community.

The Lumko Institute in South Africa is known for initiative in SCCs. Speaking at the invitation of the Catholic Bishops of India, Fr. Oswald Hirmer of the Lumko Institute for the Basic Christian Community Movement is reported to have said that the SCCs are:

> 1. Meeting in the houses; 2. Working together, i.e. Christians doing some service for each other especially for those in need in their immediate neighborhood; 3. Doing Gospel Sharing, i.e., keeping Christ in the Center, and 4. Uniting with the Universal Church by participation in its services.
>
> The SCC is not another association like the Society of Vincent DePaul, the Legion of Mary, the Charismatic Movement, etc. which are supplementary to the Church. The SCC is a miniature church. In Zambia, says Fr. Oswald, nobody can become a member of a church association unless he is a member of a SCC.
>
> Fr. Oswald says that if we remove the first characteristic—house meetings, the groups become another association. If we remove the second characteristic—working together, we get a prayer group. And if we remove the Universality of the Church—participation in its services, we become a sect.[21]

The SCCs' meetings follow a prayer format similar to the Bible study method. This method is described as follows:

> This method involves using reading the same passage from the Bible using different translations, beginning with an opening prayer. [sic]
>
> A participant reads the first passage out loud, slowly. The group reflects for about one minute, in silence, upon what word or phrase catches my attention? Then, each shares his/her word/phrase **without comment** and without adornment.
>
> Another participant reads the same passage out loud using a different translation. The group reflects for 3–5 minutes in silence on: where does this passage touch my life? Then, each participant shares, beginning with "I hear/see ..."

---

21. Reported on the website: http://www.geocities.com/orthopapism/lumko.html.

At the end, each participant prays for the person on his/her right, praying only for what that person expressed in the prior step.²²

However, in the SCCs the emphasis is not on the method but the event of people coming together in communion of faith and love in God. Besides the method, the SCCs are socially conscious of the events happening in the community and how those events affect the people, and they are also directed by the word of God and prayer to find solutions to the problems of daily living.

SCCs in the Teaching of the Roman Catholic Church

SCCs provide a way of internalizing the teaching of the universal church in the lives of the individual Christian faithful. They provide a forum where people can share with one another their understanding of the word of God as well as teachings of the church.

The SCCs are to be understood in the context of understanding the contextual nature of the church in contemporary Africa. The church after Vatican II is understood as the people of God. Referring to the various vocations in the Church and the duties accompanying the state of life of the people of God, Vatican II stated the following about the lay people in the Church:

> The term "laity" is here understood to mean all the faithful except those in Holy Orders and those who belong to a religious state approved by the Church. That is, the faithful who by Baptism are incorporated into Christ, are placed in the People of God, and in their own way share the priestly, prophetic and kingly office of Christ, and to the best of their ability carry on the mission of the whole Christian people in the Church and in the world.²³

Vatican II implies there is no Church without the lay people. There is also the idea that all people in the Church have a mission to carry out in the world. Together with those in ministerial priesthood, the laity constitutes what the 1983 Code of Canon Law terms Christ's faithful. Book II of the Code of Canon Law refers to Christ's faithful as follows:

---

22. "An African Model for Bible Study (or the Lumko method, named after the Institute which promotes it)," in the website: http://home.earthlink.net/~haywoodm/biblestudymethods.html. See also the Ignatian Method of Bible Study in the same website.
23. Flannery, "Dogmatic Constitution on the Church," no. 31.

> Christ's faithful are those who, since they are incorporated into Christ through baptism, are constituted the people of God. For this reason they participate in their own way in the priestly, prophetic, and kingly office of Christ. They are called, each according to his or her particular condition, to exercise the mission which God entrusted to the Church to fulfill in the world.[24]

SCCs are one way for Christians to nurture their faith and to realize the implications of the Christian calling in the ordinary everyday life. It is a way of realizing the call to holiness of all the Christian faithful. "Therefore all in the Church, whether they belong to the hierarchy or are cared for by it, are called to holiness, according to the apostle's saying: 'For this is the will of God, your sanctification' (1Thess 4:3; cf. Eph 1:4)."[25] The Second Vatican Council emphasized the Church's duty to open to the changing times and to the various developments in culture and in the sciences. With an awareness of the changing times, the Council fathers stated in *Gaudium et Spes*:

> New art forms adapted to our times and in keeping with the characteristics of different nations and regions should be acknowledged by the Church ... Therefore, the faithful ought to work in close conjunction with their contemporaries and try to get to know their ways of thinking and feeling, as they find them expressed in current culture. Let the faithful incorporate the findings of new sciences and teachings and the understanding of the most recent discoveries with Christian morality and thought, so that their practice of religion and their moral behavior may keep abreast of their acquaintance with science and of the relentless progress of technology: in this way they succeed in evaluating and interpreting everything with an authentically Christian sense of values.[26]

In a contextual way, therefore, the SCCs provide a way for the local churches to continually update themselves. Informed by their culture and issues affecting their lives, the members of an SCC understand the Christian gospel in a way that is relevant and thus positively transforming their community.

---

24. *The Code of Canon Law*, no 204, paragraph 1.
25. Flannery, "Dogmatic Constitution on the Church," no. 39.
26. Flannery, "Pastoral Constitution on the Church in the Modern World," no. 62.

SCCs and Social-Political Issues

The focus of the SCCs is to build the members spiritually through the word of God, the sacraments, and daily prayers. The SCCs also motivate their members to bring about transformation in the bigger community through actions informed by faith. In addition, the Christian faithful, through participation in an SCC, comes to know and appreciate the diversity of ways of life and religious pluralism in the respective society. The concern for social justice and the well being of all people is a major Christian responsibility. It is my view that SCCs provide a good forum for civic education. Through SCCs, Christians discuss various ways they can contribute to improve their society. However, care should be taken not to divide the community on the basis of partisan social and political issues. The SCCs' major task is to help the members enter into communion with one another and with the universal church, but on the other hand, Christians are not to ignore the issues that affect their day-to-day lives. SCCs can provide ways to bring about peaceful and revolutionary change informed by the Christian gospel.

SCCs can make Christians understand their civic duty, especially working for justice and peace. Civic education is meant to be a public instruction and thereby provides a way of making people aware of their responsibilities in society. For example, the Catholic Church in Kenya takes civic education as part of its mission where Christians are trained to help one another understand their responsibilities in society, such as voting for the right form of government. To do this the people should be well informed of their rights and be able to stand for those rights, especially through advocacy for good governance.

I once attended an SCC meeting where the text of St. Paul's letter to the Romans 13:1–7 was read. The debate on this text focused on verse 1, "Let every person be subordinate to the higher authorities for there is no authority except from God, and those that exist have been established by God." The questions included some such as what authority the text is referring to, because there are some people in authority out to destroy the society as opposed to building it. Are dictators willed by God? Another issue was how to reconcile Christian responsibility to help build the kingdom of God on earth, especially where political leadership is imposed on the people without popular participation through democratic voting.

Verse 7 was also discussed at length: "Pay to all their dues, taxes to whom taxes are due, toll to whom toll is due, respect to whom respect is due, honor to whom honor is due." Verse 7 was viewed as answering the questions that arose from verse 1. Verse 7 was even understood as a basis for civil disobedience and a concern was raised that an unjust or corrupt political authority need not be obeyed. Hence, corrupt leadership was thought as not commanding honor, respect, and that in an extreme case people can protest by not paying taxes to such an authority.

From the above the SCCs can be said to provide a way for the Christian faithful to actively engage their respective societies. The Christian believer who understands him or herself as a member of society and with a mission to help bring about the kingdom of God on earth will actively participate in nation building by promoting the common good and helping eliminate oppressive structures in a society. A community working well together is viewed as resonating in perfect harmony, and from a Christian perspective, this is the work of the Holy Spirit working in the lives of the people. Theological study is done in the Christian community and contributes to the strengthening of the faith in the Christian community.

PART THREE

An Evaluation of Some Contemporary Theological Methods from the Perspective of SCCs

The SCCs are concerned with communion of life and well-being of all people in their respective communities. Their concern is practical and cannot, therefore, be limited to a theological method. However, the developments in theological study can make a contribution to their evolving in terms of self-understanding and their connection to the universal communion of the Christian faith. Theological methods can also be used in analyzing the reality of the SCCs and making suggestions on new ways of being a Christian community.

The SCCs' method of sharing the word of God can be compared to the theological method of correlation. They take a passage from the Bible and relate it to the events of the people's lives and society. The word of God is a way through which the members of SCCs get the meaning or significance of God in the events of their lives. A cultural issue becomes a way of understanding God's presence in the life of the community, and alternatively, the word of God becomes a means of understanding the cultural event. In a correlative way, the SCCs foster an understanding of the people's relationship with God and with one another. God is perceived as present, and the community is taken as a sign of God's presence. The words of the gospel come to mind: "*For where two or three are gathered together in my name, there I am in the midst of them*" (Matt 18:20).

Below I consider the SCCs as a basis for evaluating and understanding various theological methods. The analysis here is shaped by my pastoral experience and theological training. Further, theological methods are presented as potentially helpful in the development of SCCs. These methods include the liberation, anthropological, and historical approaches.

Liberation Method

The liberation method can bring to the SCCs an understanding of the Christian responsibility in terms of transformative action. The community in liberation theology should be geared toward *praxis*. SCCs provide a forum for raising questions on poverty, good governance, human rights, and other issues concerning the well-being of a people in society.

The SCCs can be referred to as an embodiment of the realization of the maxim, "Power to the people," albeit without violence. They can illuminate the wider society with an understanding that change begins from the heart. The Christian view is that spiritual conversion to God leads to the good deeds of love, justice, and peace. Through the SCC, the people learn to care for and love others equally to the love of self.

At the core of SCCs is the understanding that all people belong together as members of society. The role of the Christian faithful in society is based on the understanding of communion as the nature of the Christian life within the Church and the rest of the universe—hence the mission of the Christian faithful to be light and salt of the earth (Matt 5:13–16). The Christian community, therefore, in its small ways works and prays for the well-being of all people.

The significance of liberation in an African context is brought to bear fruits through SCCs. As noted before, the struggle for liberation is indigenous to Africa, and SCCs can add a Christian dimension to the struggle for human liberation. African traditional religions offered sacrifices to the deities and spirits asking for intervention in natural catastrophes such as drought, famine, or diseases. The sacrifices symbolized the connection between a community, the spirits, and the divine. Human prosperity, in many African ethnic groups, was viewed as the result of God's or the spirits' benevolence. From the colonization of Africa by Europe, there have always been efforts or movements by Africans to free themselves from foreign domination. These struggles for political and cultural independence picked up momentum after the Second World War. However, there have always been conflicts on how to reconcile on the one hand European colonization of Africa and on the other hand the religion of Christianity with its European heritage.

African independence movements devised a way to embrace the Christian message of redemption while at the same time rejecting and fighting against colonialism. For example, the African independent churches were established as a way of ridding the Christian faith and gospel of its colonial heritage. They wanted to embrace Christ but needed to eliminate colonialism. The concern was an understanding of the irreconcilable nature of the redeeming message of Christianity and some of its messengers, who justified colonialism and its evils. The conflict was on whether there was a distinction between Christianity and colonialism. Some Christian missionaries were civil servants of the colonial governments. For example, Elizabeth Isichei writes:

> There was, as we shall see, a tradition of missionary criticism of white administrators and settlers. There have been times when the missionary critic was the only one there was. But, where there is a large settler community, there has always been a tendency for the missionary to turn into a colonial vicar. In 1919, the Anglican bishops of Mombassa and Uganda and the head of the Presbyterian mission to the Kikuyu wrote in support of forced labor: "for work of national importance." Soon afterwards, this measure became law. Frank Weston, a fiery Anglo-Catholic, wrote a pamphlet, *The Serfs of Great Britain*, furiously denouncing it and came to England to campaign.[27]

The central message of Christianity is that Jesus Christ is the redeemer of the world. But Christianity was abused as a means of socio-political and economic domination. The struggle to reconcile Christianity and foreign subjugation remains a major concern in contemporary Africa.

The theological method of liberation takes as its starting point the dehumanizing situation of poverty and oppression in Africa. From a liberation perspective, some African theologians suggest that the Christian message cannot be meaningful without addressing issues of alienation

---

27. Isichei, *A History of Christianity*, 233.

in an African context. These issues include concern for social justice and peace.

For example, from her experience of solidarity living in an Ujamaa village in Tanzania as a missionary nun, Sr. Marie Giblin states:

> Jesus' incarnation was not complete on the day of his birth. We realize from our own experience that one does not become a whole person on the day of birth; rather, it is a life-long process of growth in love and responsibility. Jesus shared in this process—he lived our life with all its limitations, pain and disappointment. He shared our human growth and freedom and knew the difficulties and joys of human relationships. Finally in Gethsemane he accepted his death—his most radical acceptance of his humanity. None of it was easy for Jesus as it is not easy for any of us.[28]

Sr. Giblin understands the Incarnation as the basis for solidarity with the poor and living with them in community. "The Word was made flesh, he lived among us" (John 1:14). In Ujamaa villages, the true nature of the Church is realized. The word of God takes flesh in these small Christian communities.[29]

Although it is my view that the quest for human liberation is indigenous to Africa, some theologians have argued that African liberation theology relies on the method of Latin American liberation theology. Robert J. Schreiter sums up liberation theology as follows:

> Put theologically, liberation models are keenly concerned with salvation. Liberation models analyze the lived experience of a people to uncover the forces of oppression, struggle, violence, and power. They concentrate on the conflictual elements oppressing a community or tearing it apart. In the midst of grinding poverty, political violence, deprivation of rights, discrimination, and hunger, Christians move from social analysis to finding echoes in the biblical witness in order to understand the struggle in which they are engaged or to find direction for the future. Liberation models concentrate on the need for change.[30]

---

28. Giblin, "Ujamaa Village Apostolate," 44.
29. Ibid.
30. Schreiter, *Constructing Local Theologies*, 15.

And further, "The special strength of liberation models has been what can happen when the realities of a people are genuinely and intimately coupled with the saving Word of God."[31]

Among the names constantly referred to in liberation theology are included, among others, Gustavo Gutiérrez and Leonardo Boff. In Latin American theology, liberation implies making a preferential option for the poor. It consists of empowering and bringing the poor in the mainstream to be the shapers of their destinies. The poor are viewed as subjects who can bring about a transformation to their situation of deprivation. According to Gutiérrez, theology is critical reflection on praxis. In theological study, "We also refer to a clear and critical attitude regarding economic and socio-cultural issues in the life and reflection of the Christian community. To disregard these is to deceive both oneself and others."[32] He holds that "theology is reflection, a critical attitude. Theology follows; it is the second step."[33] He points out that pastoral activity of the church does not flow as a conclusion from theological premises. Neither does theology produce pastoral activity; rather, it reflects upon it. Theology for Gutiérrez must be able to find in pastoral activity the presence of the Spirit inspiring the action of the Christian community.[34] Gutiérrez is critical of developmental policies in poor countries for having no achievements and not attacking the root of evils.[35] Instead of development, Gutiérrez suggests liberation. He states:

> To characterize the situation of the poor countries as dominated and oppressed leads one to speak of economic, social, and political liberation. But we are dealing here with a much more integral and profound understanding of human existence and its historical future. A broad and deep aspiration for liberation inflames the history of mankind in our day, liberation from all impediments to the exercise of his freedom . . . we must beware of all kinds of imitations as well as new forms of imperialism (rich countries).[36]

---

31. Ibid.
32. Gutiérrez, *A Theology of Liberation*, 11. See also Boff, *New Evangelization*, 11.
33. Gutiérrez, *A Theology of Liberation*, 11.
34. Ibid., 11–12.
35. Ibid., 21–27.
36. Ibid., 27.

Method in African Theology

The liberation method in theology is concerned with issues negatively affecting human existence and thereby aims to bring about the inescapable moment of radical change, which is foreign in the ordinary use of the term development.[37] "To conceive of history as a process of the liberation of man is to consider freedom as a historical conquest; it is to understand that the step from an abstract to a real freedom is not taken without a struggle against all the forces that oppress man."[38]

The method of liberation theology seems to offer a tool for critically analyzing issues in an African theological setting. However, we should not uncritically transplant the Latin American liberation theology and its Latin American social-political setting into an African historical and cultural setting. The two, African and Latin American contexts, are distinct in their own particularities.

As Schreiter points out, liberation theology is not without criticism. He notes that liberation approaches are criticized as being better at hearing the cries of the people than at listening to the biblical witness or to the testimonies of other churches. Further, the powerful tool of special analysis that is the Marxist model is tied to anti-religious and oppressive societies historically. The other weakness of liberation is that it is accused of focusing on evil instead of manifestations of grace.[39]

Additionally, SCCs, though also related to liberation theology, would critique the proponents of liberation theology by showing that human living in community is more comprehensive than presented in liberation theology. The SCCs do not emphasize one element of the Christian faith, namely praxis as in liberation theology, but emphasize the well-being of the whole human person: body, mind, and soul. While recognizing the need for praxis to bring about transformation in a situation of suffering, oppression, poverty, and alienation, SCCs also promote the spiritual and sacramental living in the church.

Anthropological Method

Some theological methods begin by analyzing what it means to be a human person. The understanding of human personality is viewed as a way of dealing with the question of God as it relates to human existence. On

---

37. Ibid.
38. Ibid., 32.
39. Schreiter, *Constructing Local Theologies*, 15.

the other hand, it can also be said that the knowledge of the human person has also been viewed as leading to an understanding of God.[40]

The theological method that lays its foundation on an African anthropology usually begins by establishing how human beings understand themselves in the context of the community life as guided by African traditional religions. African traditional religions are viewed as centered on the people's everyday life, which involves the interaction between the people and the spiritual world and God. The people understand themselves, their heritage, and their experiences in connection to the physical and spiritual world. Just as human beings are related to one another in their communities, so also they think of themselves as connected to God and the spiritual world. An anthropological method provides a tool for understanding the African traditions and religions, and this also acts as a foundation for dialogue with the Christian theological tradition and ultimately leads to the development of an African theology. However, an African anthropology is not glued to the past but continues to flow from contemporary reality in African societies. There is always progress and change in a people's culture and customs and from this development, theology acquires its dynamism and significance.

The anthropological method emphasizes that theology proceeds from the understanding of what it means to be a human being. The question of God is located in the context of the dynamism of human living. Using an anthropological method, some African theologians take an African understanding of the human person as their starting point. In African theology, Charles Nyamiti is notable in his emphasis on the African understanding of human personality as the beginning and foundation of doing theology. Nyamiti is known for his contribution in the ancestor-Christology. He argues that Jesus is our ancestor in Africa. Viewing Jesus as the ancestor is viewed by Nyamiti as a way of showing that Jesus is an African with the Africans. Nyamiti has also shown that the theology of the Trinity can also be developed from the African belief in the ancestors.[41]

The theological influence of Thomas Aquinas is present today both in the West and in Africa. Aquinas' understanding of the human person as capable of knowledge in the sensible world and ultimately the knowledge

---

40. For example, it is Karl Rahner's idea that "the history of salvation and revelation is also a history of man's systematic reflection on himself as a free being" ("Theological Anthropology," 178).

41. Nyamiti, "African Christologies Today," 11.

Method in African Theology

of God has helped shape theological investigations.[42] He attributes the knowledge of God in human beings as having its source in the created natural world as well as through divine revelation. He referred to cardinal virtues (temperance, justice, prudence, and fortitude) as realizable through human powers and theological virtues of faith, hope, and charity as possible through the intervention of God's grace.[43] Aquinas' theory of the natural law has extensive influence in theology and philosophy as well as in social sciences and jurisprudence. By the natural law, Aquinas argues that human persons are capable of distinguishing what is morally good and to be done from what is morally evil and to be avoided.[44]

The written work of St. Thomas Aquinas show how human life and living cannot be understood without at the same time understanding it as coming from God. Aquinas' work is structured in such a way to show human beings as coming forth from God and also as returning to God. God is the end toward whom all creatures return.[45] In the work of Aquinas, the possibility of human knowledge is connected with the possibility of humans coming to the natural knowledge of God. The influence of Aquinas has been evident in the Roman Catholic theology for centuries. African theology also cannot escape the intellectual genius of Thomas Aquinas.

Karl Rahner also should be understood from the perspective of transcendental Thomism. According to Thomas Aquinas, God is pure act, the simple being who is one. He is the cause of the existence of all beings. Rahner's transcendental approach to theology gives the possibility of an open, not closed, way of doing theology. The nature of the human subject makes it possible to have the knowledge of God. From a transcendental point of view, any positive statement we make about human beings is ultimately a statement about God and vice versa. To know God is to know ourselves. A transcendental subject makes it possible for a theology of grace. Rahner states, "All theology stands in need of this transcen-

---

42. See the *Summa Contra Gentiles*, Chapter XXV. Aquinas states, "Now, seeing that all creatures, even those that are devoid of reason, are directed to God as their last end, and that all reach this end in so far as they have some share of a likeness to Him, the intellectual creature attains to Him in a special way, namely, through its proper operation, by understanding Him. Consequently this must be the end of the intellectual creature, namely, to understand God" (Pegis, *Introduction to Aquinas*, 442–43).

43. Aquinas, *Summa Theologiae*, I–II qq. 49 (a. 4), 51, 54 (a. 2–3), 55 (a. 1–4), 56 (a. 1), 57 (a. 2–5), 58 (a. 1–2), 60 (a. 1), 61 (a. 1–2), 62, 63, 64 (a. 1–2).

44. Ibid., q. 94, a. 2.

45. Aquinas, *Summa Contra Gentiles*, chapter XXV.

dental and anthropological change of direction because all theology is dependent upon the mutually determining doctrines of the Trinity, Grace and Incarnation, and these doctrines today require a transcendental approach."[46] The understanding of the human subject as having an infinite capacity makes all theology possible. The subject has the capability of conscious self-reflection, which begins from everyday experience and in a special way the faith experience. In Rahner, the question about God must begin with the question about human beings.[47] Clearly, Rahner's theology seems to provide a vantage point from which to view other theological methods. From the transcendental Thomism of Rahner, one can evaluate other theologies in the twentieth and twenty-first centuries.

Christian theology always has the task of rethinking the faith in changed times. In his theology, Rahner confronts the medieval scholastic philosophy of Thomas Aquinas and Neo-Thomistic theology with the problems and questions of modern philosophy, especially as formulated by Immanuel Kant in his critical and transcendental philosophy. The theology of Karl Rahner has had much influence in seminary and Catholic university education in many places in the world. Rahner's work is concerned with the central problem of philosophy: the nature and possibility of metaphysics, and the question of possibility of a speculative and rational theology. This features prominently in *the Spirit in the World*.[48]

The work of Karl Rahner is also a good example of an anthropological method in theological study. According to Rahner, an authentic anthropology is viewed as leading to a good theology. It is a theology that is centered on the human subject. Further, in Rahner's work, "a transcendental line of inquiry . . . is present when and to the extent that it raises the question of the conditions in which knowledge of a specific subject is possible in the knowing subject himself."[49]

The human person for Rahner is the subject who has an infinite capacity for knowledge from the context of being or all reality that exists. Being constitutes all there is to know, and only God constitutes "Being" in the fullest sense. The absolute being is the sufficient reason or the efficient

---

46. Rahner, "Theology and Anthropology," 37.
47. Weger, *Karl Rahner: An Introduction to His Theology*, 37.
48. Fiorenza, "Introduction: Karl Rahner and the Kantian Problematic," xix.
49. Rahner, "Reflections on Methodology in Theology," 86.

Method in African Theology

cause of human transcendence. Without God, human transcendence is thought to have no meaning and could not be possible by itself.

The theological method of Rahner, therefore, can be categorized as the "turn to the subject." On the theology of Rahner, Anne Carr states, "A theological anthropology could emerge only after the 'turn to the subject' of modern philosophy and hence 'a systematic anthropology corresponding to the knowledge man has attained of himself as a subject . . .'"[50] It presupposes the historical giving and hearing of revelation. It is *posteriori* and yet *a priori* in that it comes from God. This would include considering the meaning of human creatureliness, specifically created personal subjectivity as an unlimited receptivity for God. Theological anthropology necessarily, therefore, develops the meaning of human historicity that consists of intrinsic human relation to the world, the structures of the corporeal, social, and sexual determinations, and the difference between human essence and existence.[51] ". . . Rahner's theology of mystery and symbol, indicating the union between history and transcendence, lies at the foundation of the whole of his theology and is the meaning of theological anthropology."[52] Theological anthropology as a method means the elucidation of the connections between dogma (broadly conceived) and human experience.[53] This way Rahner rejects the extrinsic character of the post-Tridentine Catholic understanding of grace as a superstructure on a human nature already complete in itself.[54]

For its foundation, African theology also claims to proceed from an understanding of human life and its relation to God in an African context. Since theology is an attempt to understand human life and God, African theology has to evolve this understanding in an African worldview. The Christian understanding of a human person as created in the image and the likeness of God provides a sound theological starting point. From Genesis the human person is viewed as pointing to the creator God (Gen 1:26–27). The glory of creation leads to the consideration of the glory of the creator.

---

50. Carr, *The Theological Method of Karl Rahner*, 179.
51. Ibid., 180.
52. Ibid., 191.
53. Ibid., 193.
54. Ibid., 195.

Without forgetting that there is no human existence without God, the SCCs proceed from an understanding of what it means to be a human being in community. The sacred Scriptures provide a valuable starting point for understanding the nature of humanity. Human beings were created in the image and the likeness of God (Gen 1:26–27). SCCs provide a forum for the promotion of human dignity by promoting the social and religious nature of human existence. This human dignity is promoted in an integral way. The well-being of all people has to be thought of in terms of both spiritual and material nature. Human beings are embodied souls; the human body and soul define what it is to be a human being. The human person is always in relationship with God, the world, and with other human persons.

Undoubtedly, as stated above, the SCCs have a foundation on a sound anthropology. SCCs are derived from an understanding of the communal or relational nature of human existence. They are based on the people's faith in God, who is the creator of all things on earth and in heaven, visible and invisible. Human welfare is considered a way of fostering faith in God. As a communion of the faithful, the SCCs have their foundation in the members' profession and practice of faith. Hence, the celebration of the sacraments is the worship of the one God—Father, Son, and the Holy Spirit as professed in the Christian creed.

The understanding of the Trinitarian and sacramental faith of the Church would also benefit from an anthropological study. A cultural reference enhances the understanding of symbolism of the sacraments. And thus the local human expression of joy is incorporated in the liturgical celebrations, thereby making it possible to understand the salvific power of the paschal mystery of Jesus Christ as taking place in time in the community of faith. I have always been impressed by the celebration of the Eucharist in many parishes I have visited in Kenya where instead of ringing of the bell at the consecration of the Eucharist when the host is raised, there is an ululation and a song from the congregation, making the celebration a joyous community affair.

Understanding the human person as promoted by the anthropological method in theology is commendable. However, the anthropological method as developed by theologians like Karl Rahner pay much attention to the transcendental powers of human personhood, such as capacity for knowledge and moral decisions, while showing little concern for the cultural and historical context in which human beings gain the knowledge of self and ultimately come to faith in God. On the other hand, the SCCs simply understand life in the social context of the members while addressing the social concerns of the community.

Historical Method

The Christian life in any SCC has its foundation in the people's faith in Jesus Christ as the son of God and the savior of the world. For this reason, there is the perennial need for a catechesis based on a good Christology. In the SCCs, the Christian faithful reflect on the word of God in their historical situation. Their response to the events of their lives is informed by the word of God and the sacraments of the church. The SCCs are embodied by the members' understanding of God as the center of their lives and thereby, the call to shape their lives in faith according to God's will. Faith in Jesus Christ as the savior of the world binds together all the members of the SCCs. And therefore, no matter what sufferings and pain the believers go through, they know, as it is in Gikuyu language, that, "*muhonokia wa thi*" (the savior of the world) out of love died for them and continually intervenes to save all people from their troubles.

In an African setting, history provides the means for critical theological analyses. It is only from a historical setting that theology can have meaning and relevance. This historical understanding is especially poignant in an African context. The historical method views an understanding of history as impacting theological thought. A historically conscious method is necessary in African theology. There is no way one can develop a sound African theology without studying in depth the African cultures and history.

History is not just concerned with events from the past. It is concerned with past as it affects the present. Since history is the progress of a people over time, new events present a new challenge and opportunity for intellectual thought and social action. In an African setting, history is not to be viewed as cut-and-dry phenomena but a continuous progress of human beings in community and their encounters with their universe. A sound African theology analytically and critically engages itself with the ever-changing historical situation. The SCCs provide a concrete way in which a community engages itself with what is happening and therefore, engages issues as they take place.

When I say that African theology is historical, I mean that it is about people. Any theology that does not concern itself with people becomes irrelevant. Christian teachings are also addressed to people of all times, but any people understand it in their own time and place. The preceding can also be said of any religious teachings—that they are derived from a people's practice of their faith, a faith nourished by the events of their life and the attempt to understand the significance of those events. If theology is people-centered, there should be no conflict between what contributes to humans' journey of self-fulfillment and religious teaching. The problem in Africa, since the time of the early missionaries, has been to isolate Christian message from the African traditional customs and background of the believer. Traditional customs were viewed as contrary to the Christian gospel and condemned simply as heathen practices. Some have even used the imagery of light and darkness to refer to Christian gospel and African traditional customs respectively, not to mention the insulting reference to Africa as the Dark Continent.

Sound African Christian theology has to engage and assimilate positive cultural practices and beliefs. For example, the traditional African understanding of the extended family can be helpful in understanding the nature of the Church as a community.

However, in the endeavor of developing a historically conscious African theology, African theologians are also open to other non-African theologians, especially those who have extensively developed the historical method in theology. An example of a historical method would be the European political theology of a theologian such as Johann Baptist Metz. Christian faith is historical in nature. Christianity is founded on the historical person of Jesus: his life, public ministry, suffering, death, and resurrection. The person who comes to believe in Jesus Christ does so in a historical and cultural setting. The message of Christ, understood and lived in a historical setting, leads to a social and historical transformation. For example, Metz is known for his concern with history in theology, especially in Germany after the Second World War. Metz continually raised the question of where the Church was during the time of National Socialism and the holocaust in Germany. In the work of Metz, solidarity with the poor emerges as a key-word. He also incorporates the idea of solidarity between rich nations of the north with the so-called third world countries of the South.

Metz's historical method is comparable in many ways with the liberation method. As in liberation theology, Metz's political and historical method suggests a way of studying theology that addresses social ills in society. Metz writes:

> The history of the biblical religion is a history of the way in which a people and the individuals belonging to that people became subjects in the presence of their God ... Those men were called out of the anxieties and compulsions of archaic societies in order to become subjects of a new historical process. The terms of their state as subjects were dynamic—being called in danger, being called out of fear, the exodus, conversion, the raising up of their head, the imitation of their leader and so on. Religion was not an additional phenomenon. It was an active part of the process by which Israel became a subject. In the Old Testament, it was in the exodus that the People most clearly became subjects.[55]

The human relationship with God, Metz argues, is not a slavish relationship but one in which human beings are subjects actively engaged with their life and destiny. History or what Metz calls memory becomes a way of living out the transformative nature of Christian living. He explains, "It is obvious that the category of memory—in the form of a memory of suffering—and the category of narrative—as a linguistic identification of the stories of human suffering, which escape the system of the history of progress and triumph—is given greater importance ... similarly, the category of solidarity in its extended sense of anamnesis or the memory of the sacrifices of history also gains in importance."[56]

In Metz's work, the main concepts of fundamental theology are praxis and subject.[57] According to Metz, "Practical fundamental theology is ... directly opposed to a non-dialectical subordination of praxis to theory or idea."[58] For Metz, "All Christology is nourished, for the sake of its own truth, by praxis and particularly the praxis of the imitation of Christ. It is in other words, expressed in a practical knowledge, ... all Christology is subject to the primacy of praxis."[59] Further, he describes praxis thus:

> Christian praxis as social praxis continues to be determined by an excess of historical determinations that are the non-inference function of the prevailing social reality. This is where the herme-

55. Metz, *Faith in History and Society*, 60–61.
56. Ibid., 58.
57. Ibid., 49.
58. Ibid., 50.
59. Ibid., 51.

neutics of memory as a dangerous phenomenon or as subversion and rebellion plays an indispensable part. Every utopian concept of liberation which questions and breaks through what is currently held to be plausible is ultimately rooted in this kind of memory, which is in turn not simply a reflection or reproduction of the contemporary factors determining society and economics.[60]

From Metz's point of view, the Church has a social nature, "... as a historical and social reality, the church is always active as a political factor."[61] In Metz's theology, there is a connection between the Christian message and the modern world.

Remembering Christ's love is a "dangerous and at the same time liberating memory that oppresses and questions the present because it reminds us not of some open future, but precisely this future and because it compels Christians constantly to change themselves so that they are able to take this future into account."[62] Metz suggests a "spirituality and the formation of spirituality in the church as a spirituality of liberated freedom which bears witness to and justifies in the extension of a freedom that is critical of society ... [in the south] the witness borne by this freedom will take the form above all of a courageous struggle against social misery."[63] He calls cultic spirituality opium of the intellectuals (middle class). Dangerous memories make demands on people. The history of suffering is a history of guilt and the exonerating mechanism of an abstract-total emancipation.[64] Narrative is practical as story telling.[65] Solidarity is above all a category of help, support, and togetherness by which the subject, suffering acutely and threatened, can be raised up.[66] He calls for world-wide solidarity.

In its concerns, African theology has a historical responsibility. From Metz's concept of dangerous memories, African theology can show its practical relevance in transforming situations of suffering and misery to ones of hope and love. Theology, most of all in Africa, has a prophetic mission. It should challenge systems that propagate conditions of social

60. Ibid., 56.
61. Ibid., 89.
62. Ibid., 90.
63. Ibid., 94.
64. Ibid., 124.
65. Ibid., 195.
66. Ibid., 229.

alienation and oppression. The prophetic voice is one that proclaims freedom to those oppressed by unjust historical social-political structures.

The historical method in theology has a trans-cultural nature. History is an important tool in theological study; otherwise theology would appear to be irrelevantly out of touch with reality. For example, in African theology Bénézet Bujo uses a historical method to show the coming of Christianity in Africa and how this event affected the traditional way of life in Africa.[67]

Conclusion

The theological methods of liberation, anthropology, and the historical approach applied in an African context constitute the process of inculturation of the Christian gospel. The SCCs provide a basis for understanding what inculturation is all about. Without saying that they are inculturating the Christian faith, the members of SCCs achieve the goal of inculturation, which is living their Christian lives in a particular cultural-historical setting. SCCs foster dialogue based on faith and culture. They are a means for helping people see the significance of their faith in their cultural context. Through creative imagination, in song and dance, and in communion of love with one another, the members of SCCs understand their Christian faith and its significance in the wider society.

In this section, the SCCs are presented as a way of evaluating the strengths and weaknesses of some theological methods. Although no theological method is adequate in itself, the SCCs provide a testing field for the relevance of theological inquiry. The discussion in this work sees the possibility of one theological method somehow being supplemented by other theological methods and thereby promoting an appreciation of interdependence of various approaches. A theological method can be compared to a point of view, and no one viewpoint is self-sufficient considering the diversity in the world. The SCCs provide a hermeneutical tool for analyzing theological developments as well as a way to demonstrate their significance (or insignificance) to Christian living.

Christian life presupposes the Christological foundation. In the next chapter, the Christological foundation in African inculturation theology is considered.

---

67. See Bujo, *African Theology in its Social Context*, 59.

4

The Christological Foundation in African Inculturation Christian Theology

THE MAJOR ISSUE IN African Christian theology is developing an African understanding of the gospel and the person of Jesus Christ. A number of theologians who have contributed in the making of an African Christology will be considered in this section. These theologians include Charles Nyamiti, Bénézet Bujo, Jean Marc Ela, and Laurenti Magesa. Christology is the major area of African Christian theology that is more developed than any other theological area, such as biblical studies, ecclesiology, moral theology, or even sacramental theology. But Christology binds together all other theological areas of study since biblical studies, ecclesiology, and sacramentology are all based on the person and the salvific action of Jesus Christ: his life, his public ministry, and his suffering, death, and resurrection. However, some of the Christological theologies developing in Africa will be seen as further complicating what is otherwise a simple Christian message.

Is There an African Christology? Africa is one of the continents in the world where Christianity has flourished in a very rapid way.[1] The very presence of so many people who believe in Jesus Christ calls for a deeper understanding and development of the theological study of the Christian faith.

The message of the New Testament is that in Jesus of Nazareth, God had become a human being. In African Christian theology, coming after Vatican Council II in the Roman Catholic Church, the emphasis has been to view Jesus as a member of the African community. African Christian theology is mainly concerned with the development of an articulate African Christology. For example, commenting on the contributors to

---

1. See *World Almanac*, 695.

The Christological Foundation in African Inculturation Christian Theology

the symposium held in Nairobi, Kenya, in March 1989, and from which the book came, the editors, Mugambi and Magesa, made the following introductory remarks:

> From the perspective of each author's own expertise, all of the papers attempted to deliberate on the specific significance of Christ as seen by Africans, particularly by African Christians, at the present stage of their appropriation, understanding and appreciation of Him and faith in Him. The basic question in the whole endeavor was, once again: Who and what is Jesus the Christ in and for the Africa of today? This symposium was a week of recalling symbols, idioms and appropriate expressions from the African experience, which will carry the message of the Gospel more effectively both today and tomorrow.[2]

The main concern of an African theology is to promote an understanding of the Christian message in an African setting. This task involves thinking about the mystery of Christ in African realities and thought categories. This is made clear by the Tanzanian Bishop Christopher Mwoleka. On the church and small Christian communities, Bishop Mwoleka states:

> What we need is to manifest religion more faithfully and more honestly in earnest. To manifest it in a way which is less concealing and which truly reveals what is essential to Christianity. A way that lays bare the REALITY of what Christianity is, so that everybody may see and witness for himself the plenitude of the NEW LIFE IN CHRIST; that is many persons sharing one and the same life; persons revealing "the authentic face of God and religion." Only then can the Church be truly a sign and a witness of the Kingdom of God in the world.[3]

As a result, some African theologians, especially those studied later in this section, have suggested that Jesus should be understood as brother, king, ancestor, and proto-ancestor, among others. However, the theological view of Christ as the ancestor in Africa is a dominant theme in African Christology. Hence, one cannot justifiably ignore the theological view of Jesus Christ as ancestor/proto-ancestor. Toward this end, the question on the accuracy of referring to Jesus as an African ancestor will be raised. My view is that to promote an understanding of Jesus as an African ancestor

---

2. Mugambi and Magesa, "Introduction," xi.
3. Mwoleka, "Small Christian Communities and Human Promotion," 19.

complicates the message of the incarnation of Jesus Christ, the second person of the Holy Trinity. A suggestion is made that it is far easier to understand the person of Jesus Christ in an African context—simply put, from the perspective of contemporary African understanding of what it means to be a human being. The preceding leads to the proposal that an African Christology can use scholarly study of the historical Jesus as a basis of how Christianity expresses its faith through existing and current cultural practices.

The task of an African Christian theology is to lay a solid foundation on the person and ministry of Christ. Unfortunately, this task has not been accomplished, since African theology is still at a preliminary stage of trying to define its identity, goals, and scope. In an African context this is possible only through a Christology that has significance to African reality and human living. For example, from his research in Uganda, John Waliggo has pointed out the significance of a contextual and experiential Christology. For African Christians, Waliggo states: "In sum, the Christ identified is the tangible, functional, African and dynamic Christ with whom they can fully and at all times feel at home."[4] Hence, we can highlight that there is need for an African Christology with the goal of enriching and diversifying other theologies in a multi-cultural world and not simply promoting sectarianism in Christianity.

PART ONE

The Making of an African Christology: Is Jesus Christ the African Ancestor?

The section explores the work of various African theologians and their approaches to African Christology. Questions are raised on their Christological method as well as suggestions made in the development of an African Christology. An analysis of African Christology in the works of Charles Nyamiti, Bénézet Bujo, Jean Marc Ela, and Laurenti Magesa is important because these are a few among theologians who have made a major contribution in the development of theology in Africa, especially in the Roman Catholic theology. While Nyamiti's concern is to develop an African systematic understanding of the Trinitarian theology, Bujo and Magesa develop an African Christology as the foundation of an African

---

4. Waliggo, "African Christology in a Situation of Suffering," 107.

moral theology. The three theologians, in their studies, have postulated the ancestorhood of Jesus Christ as the basis of an African understanding of the Christian message. It is important, therefore, to briefly analyze the work of Nyamiti, Bujo, and Magesa. Ela concentrates on issues of poverty, oppression, and suffering. He suggests that any African theology has to deal with the liberation of the people. The analysis in this work will be concerned primarily with how these theologians have developed an African Christology as a foundation of their theology. However, since these theologians are active in their theological endeavors, I wish to admit that any analyses of their theological works can only be tentative since their theology is open to further developments.

Further, claiming Jesus as an African ancestor will be viewed as raising concerns on how to reconcile the particularity of Jesus Christ as a historical person. Jesus was born a Jew in the first century in Palestine. Christian faith teaches that in Jesus of Nazareth the Son of God became a human being. The faith of the early Church is that Jesus is Lord. He is the savior. He is God. The claim in African theology that Jesus is the African ancestor par excellence or the Proto-Ancestor will be seen to raise some questions in the understanding of the Incarnation.

Charles Nyamiti: The Making of an African Systematic Theology

Charles Nyamiti has been a teacher at the Catholic University of Eastern Africa in Nairobi, Kenya, since its inception in 1984. CUEA, as the university is popularly called, has been over the years a meeting point for African scholars from various backgrounds. The CUEA website indicates he is now an *emeritus* professor.[5]

Nyamiti describes African Christian theology as the understanding and expression of the Christian faith in accordance with African needs and mentality, for which there are two methods of approach, namely inculturation and liberation theology.[6] African theology is based on an African understanding of human personality. However, Nyamiti holds that a human person in Africa is to be understood in the context of the African past. According to Nyamiti, "The elements in the African understanding of person are, in fact, coextensive with the elements found in the African traditional worldview. It is from such a vitalistic point of

---

5. See the Catholic University of Eastern Africa's website: www.cuea.edu.
6. Nyamiti, "Contemporary African Christologies," 63–64.

departure that it is possible to elaborate an African theology of the mystery of incarnation."[7] Nyamiti argues for an African anthropological foundation for his theology.

For Christology to be meaningful, Nyamiti suggests that Jesus Christ has to be understood from an African understanding of human personhood. However, Nyamiti presents an African understanding of ancestors as a foundation for understanding the incarnation of Christ. According to Nyamiti, Christ, who is seen as one of the African ancestors and greater than all of the ancestors, becomes the model of behavior for his brethren and the source of Christian tradition and its stability. Being God-man, he is ultimately more perfect as model of conduct than the African ancestor can ever be, for he is not only an extrinsic prototype of behavior for his brethren but also ultimately the source and vital principal of Christian life.[8] Hence Nyamiti has suggested that Jesus Christ should be viewed as the proto-ancestor in African theology.

The proto-ancestor, according to Nyamiti, provides a foundation for a "narrative ethic" which affirms that "if Christ is proto-ancestor, source of life and fulfillment, our conduct must model itself on re-enacting the memory of his passion, death and resurrection."[9] It is an ethic that demands personal assimilation of the experiences memorized in Christ's paschal mystery. The virtues shown in this mystery must become part of our own lives. It is a Christocentric ethic that confirms, in his view, the positive elements of African anthropocentrism, for example, on hospitality, family spirit and respect to parents, etc. It is a call therefore, to develop a system of ethics that addresses the continent's problems by reverting to these sound values in African communities. The Christ-event becomes liberating, humanizing, and purifying in the African context.[10]

In the African traditional religions, he observes that God's justice is seen in the context of God as judge who rewards the good and punishes the evil ones. Nyamiti clearly notes, ". . . African religious behavior is centered mainly on man's life in this world, with the consequences that religion is chiefly functional or a means to serve people to acquire earthly goods (life, health, fecundity, wealth, etc.), and to maintain social

---

7. Nyamiti, "African Christologies Today," 5.
8. Nyamiti, *Christ as Our Ancestor*, 9–21.
9. Ibid.
10. Ibid., 8.

cohesion and order."¹¹ And that ". . . when the African calls God 'father,' this fatherhood has to be understood as being dynamic, living and sacred—a mystical vital power that leads to living and mystical solidarity and participation in human community (of the living and the dead), for the benefit (life, power, well-being, protection, liberation, etc.) of the individual as a member of the community in living contact and solidarity with the whole cosmos."¹² Nyamiti maintains that in the African traditional religions "life is not abstractly conceived, but as concretely lived in human community and the world of nature and spirits. Fullness of life is understood as maturity comprising fecundity, practical wisdom, sacrality, rights and responsibility as well as liberty from any type of subjugation."¹³ It is obtained through vital communion with or openness (relationality) to the world of spirits (God—the Supreme Being, ancestors, and other spirits), fellow human beings, and the world of nature. Society and religion in Africa are therefore centered on the human subject.¹⁴

Nyamiti observes further that God is in some African communities seen as androgynous, that is, as male and female at the same time. It means that God is autonomous, full of strength and wholeness. It is like referring to God as ultimate reality. In some cases there could be excessive anthropomorphism where natural objects are seen as divinities.¹⁵

From the ancestral theology, Nyamiti develops an African Trinitarian theology as follows:

> With an understanding of ancestral relation it is possible to examine the inner life of God (Trinity) and discover that there is an ancestral kinship among the divine persons: the Father is the Ancestor of the Son, the Son is the Descendant of the Father. These two persons live their ancestral kinship through the Spirit whom they mutually communicate to as their ancestral Oblation and Eucharist. The Spirit is reciprocally donated not only in token of their mutual love as *Gift* but also on behalf of the homage to their reciprocal holiness (as oblation) and gratitude to their

---

11. Nyamiti, *African Tradition and the Christian God*, 11.
12. Ibid., 13.
13. Nyamiti, "The Problem of Evil in African Traditional Cultures and Today's African Inculturation and Liberation Theologies," 40.
14. Ibid., 40–41.
15. Ibid, 14–15.

beneficence to each other (as *Eucharist*, from the Greek: *eucharistein* "to thank").[16]

Nevertheless, it is somehow impossible for human beings to totally understand the inner life of God. The human mind can be said to be too small to conceive wholly the concept of the being of God. We can know something about the mystery of God, but the mystery remains a hidden or "other" to human beings.

In a generalized way, Nyamiti acknowledges the anthropocentric nature of African traditional religion. However, African ethnic groups are as diverse as the geographical diversity of the African continent. Nyamiti's work seems to homogenize a rather heterogeneous continent. African traditions and customs are plural by nature, just as the African continent is broad from one corner to the other. Nyamiti's method pays a great deal of attention to African's historical past (i.e., traditional religions) and not the contemporary African history.

Bénézet Bujo: The Making of an African Christian Ethics

African theology in Bujo's work is concerned with inculturation. Inculturation in Africa, according to Bujo, has to do with what he calls "ancestral theology."[17] "The inculturation of Christianity, however, should not hide the social relevance of African tradition, but rather challenge the African person to transform his/her world into a better place."[18] Bujo seems to suggest that the solutions to issues that concern Africa are to be found in the African past.

Bujo also views African theology as based on the African understanding of human life. According to Bujo, the African religious worldview is as follows:

> However, if life and especially human life comes from God, the African also knows that God uses his ancestors to communicate this life to him. The original ancestor continues to live in his descendants, and is, after God, at the origin of the existence of the present generation. He had transmitted his own vital force to those of his descendants who in their turn have already joined the dead, but remain nevertheless responsible for the welfare and sustenance of the life in their clan. This is the reason why every

---

16. Nyamiti, "African Christologies Today," 11.
17. Bujo, *The Ethical Dimension of Community*, 19.
18. Ibid., 19.

surviving clan member must be in close contact with the departed members of the family, of the clan, or of the tribe or nation. It will be, accordingly, the father of the family in the case of a family, in the case of the clan the senior elder of it, for the ethnic group, the chief or a similar person, for the nation, the king as the case may be, who will be the constitutional representative of the respective ancestors, and are, as such, empowered to transmit life to their respective communities, and to enforce the moral order established by the fathers.[19]

Bujo presents an hierarchical understanding of human living in an African community. But hierarchy may sound like a rigid system with no means for interpersonal dialogue. Hierarchy also does not fit into the palaver of the moral discernment process as proposed by Bujo. "Biological life is transmitted by God through the elders and ancestors. Along with this life, God and the ancestors, and the elders in their respective positions, take care to lay down rules, in the form of laws and taboos, to ensure the prosperity of the society."[20] Hence, "The African person lives within an extended family. This togetherness is based on a common ancestor who founded the community of the clan or tribe, which is composed of the living as well as the dead. The latter are indeed not dead; the dead are not really dead but are to be regarded rather as the 'living dead.'"[21]

Bujo further elaborates the black African's concept of life as hierarchical. He sees the African concept of life as "a participation in God, but it is always mediated by one standing above the recipient in the hierarchy of being. This hierarchy belongs both to the invisible and to the visible world."[22] It is very close to what Thomas Aquinas refers to as natural law and the participation in the eternal law by human persons.[23] In this hierarchy, God is first, followed by the founding fathers of the clan, tribal heroes, and deceased elders, other members of the family, and various invisible powers of the spirit world. The leaders of the community occupy a central place. The ancestors live on in their descendants, for it is a participatory concept of life.[24] In this stratum it is impossible to separate religion from

19. Bujo, *African Christian Morality at the Age of Inculturation*, 75.
20. Bujo, *African Theology in its Social Context*, 21.
21. Bujo, *The Ethical Dimension of Community*, 15.
22. Bujo, *African Theology in its Social Context*, 20.
23. Aquinas, *Summa Theologiae*, I–II, q. 91, a. 2.
24. Bujo, *African theology in its Social Context*, 20.

social-political powers in an African community. An African society is viewed as one indivisible whole. This is true considering how today in some African nations, religion and state intermingle so much that you would find leaders seeking to be sanctioned by the church for their political survival.

According to Bujo, living people should conduct themselves according to the patterns established by the ancestors, for in this way they strengthen the tribe or clan as a whole. Responsibility in the community will depend on one's status; for example, the father of a family, clan-leader, chief, and king each has an obligation to see that the right order established by God and ancestors is carefully maintained. Any offense against the laws and customs of the tribe is despising God and the ancestors. Each and every person has a role to play in strengthening the tribe, and the morality of any act is determined by its life-giving potential.[25]

From Bujo's understanding of an African view of life, it seems that the nearer a person is to the original ancestor, the more influential one is in the community. Is there not an equal value to all human life? On human life, besides the living members of the community, Bujo has included the ancestors, who he refers to as the "living dead." In an African community Bujo suggests that the "... ancestors become the locus (the human nature) where we encounter the God of salvation; and Christ becomes the unique and privileged locus of total encounter with those ancestors."[26] Ultimately, he refers to Christ as ancestor-par-excellence or proto-ancestor.[27] Christ plays the role of the ancestors because "he enables us to realize the saving future that fulfills history."[28] Christ makes the future possible. Bujo states: "Actualizing these inherited memories of our ancestors thus becomes a commemorative narrative soteriology aimed at assuring the unity of an all-inclusive (past, present, future) community—including all beneficent ancestors—that begins in this life and stretches beyond the grave."[29]

From the ancestor theology, Bujo shows that the historical Jesus gains prominence when viewed as the proto-ancestor in African theology. He explains, "If we look back on the historical Jesus of Nazareth, we can see

---

25. Ibid., 22.
26. Bujo, "A Christocentric Ethic for Black Africa," 143.
27. Ibid.
28. Ibid., 144.
29. Ibid., 143.

The Christological Foundation in African Inculturation Christian Theology

in him, not only one who lived the African ancestor-ideal in the highest degree, but one who brought that ideal to an altogether new fulfillment. Jesus worked miracles, healing the sick, opening the eyes of the blind, raising the dead to life. In short, he brought life, and life-force, in its fullness. He lived his mission for his fellow-humans in an altogether matchless way, and, furthermore, left to his disciples, as his final commandment, the law of love."[30] Bujo views morality as based on ancestral rules in an African context. Is moral discernment not a continuous process? In the theological work of Bujo, morality presupposes a community in an African context. Bujo writes: "The morality of an act is determined by its life-giving potential: good acts are those which contribute to the community's vital force, whereas bad acts, however apparently insignificant, are those which tend to diminish life. African society is a real 'mystical body', encompassing both dead and living members, in which every member has an obligation to every other."[31]

In addition, the ancestors are not divinities but are mere human beings who lived before the living human beings. The past or history of a people is also relevant in shaping their individual and societal living. Clearly, the past should not be glorified too much while forgetting the concerns of the present. The theological talk about ancestors may seem to indicate that the dead have more influence than the living members, while the elders occupy a more powerful position than younger members of a community. Today, this has spelled disaster in many African nations where the senior statesman, because of his age, has also turned out to be the most corrupt since no one should question the *Mzee*, the older man in the Kiswahili language. Age and merit should never be separated. Furthermore, all human life has its inalienable dignity.

Bujo, like Nyamiti, has pointed out that life for the African clan society is central and is considered sacred. He notes that long before the coming of Christianity into Africa, the African traditional religion(s) recognized God as the source of all life and especially human life. He says life for an African is considered "as constituting a single, undifferentiated whole."[32] Christianity for him did not consist of its proclamation of one God, for Africans knew God, but it brought a complete and definitive

---

30. Bujo, *African Theology in its Social Context*, 79.
31. Ibid., 22.
32. Ibid., 17.

proclamation of the one who is also the God of Jesus Christ.[33] What Bujo is saying is that Christianity found a fertile ground in Africa because the people already knew there was a supreme being who is the source of all things they see and the creator of all human beings.

The idea that human beings affirm the absolute being as a mystery and realize themselves through this mystery seems similar to the theology of Karl Rahner or transcendental Thomism.[34] Bujo is influenced by the theology of Thomas Aquinas.[35] Bujo refers to traditional Christian theology, which tended to split human beings into body and soul and to preach the salvation of the soul. For Africans, he observes that they could not comprehend any division of human beings but they "experienced themselves as a unity, living in a network of living relationships with God and with nature."[36] For the Africans, "All relationships, between person and person, living and dead, and between persons and nature, are rooted in God and point towards God and towards the end of all things in God. God cannot be imagined without God's creation, not without God's saving will for mankind."[37] Furthermore, it is from experience that people also come to know what is wrong and what is right, what harms life and what enhances it.

Although, Bujo has emphasized the role of the ancestors in an African moral life, his Christian ethics seem to have a foundation in a generalized view of human nature. For Bujo, what is normatively human, those human traits, habits, and acts that promote human flourishing, is the foundation of an African ethics. Right conduct contributes to the community's vital force, and bad acts diminish life in the African context. Consequently, Bujo has argued that African worldview is anthropocentric, not in the sense that there is no place for God, but that human life is ultimately God's gift. Hence, focusing on life is focusing on God.[38] Initiation rites in this context become like ordination ceremonies where the young people are consecrated with their procreative power into the whole community

---

33. Ibid., 18.

34. Rahner, *Foundations of Christian Faith*, 75–79.

35. For example, Bujo wrote his habilitation on St. Thomas Aquinas and it was published as *Die Begründung des Sittlichen*.

36. Bujo, *African theology in its Social Context*, 32.

37. Ibid., 32.

38. Ibid., 23.

of the living and the dead, "But (also) consecrated to the creator God and to the ancestors, from whom flow all life and strength."[39]

From this perspective by Bujo, human sexuality is seen in the African traditions as a means for continuity of the clan. He argues that procreation is the key for an African understanding of sexuality and for this reason childlessness and celibacy were viewed as a sin against the community. This explains why we have so many "trial marriages," for the achievement of life (childbearing) is an affair of the whole community and thereby very serious. A marriage is required to be sanctioned by the community before being taken to the church. It is usually the parents who have to bless the couple that is to be sacramentally wed in the church; hence, honoring the parents is connected to the cult of the ancestors.[40] However, this seems to emphasize one goal of marriage, namely the procreative end, at the expense of other ends of marriage, such as love and companionship.

Bujo has shown that African views of the past (history) are very important in the process of developing an African theology. The religious perspective of Africa is comparable to what is referred to as "narrative theology," which has its roots in the Bible. From the African traditions, one has a rich heritage from which to choose life-giving actions and words of the ancestors or not. It is choosing that path that leads to life or death. Sin and evil originate from human beings. "The moral order is thus seen as a matter, not of the relation between human beings and God, but of the relationships between human beings themselves."[41] The common good of the society is at the center of all considerations of what is good or bad. In many African communities, any individual who threatened the life and well being of a community was cast out. For example, in many African tribes in the past sorcerers, murderers, and thieves were executed, for they were harming the well-being of the community. But extra-judicial execution would constitute a criminal act in many nations in contemporary Africa. Property rights were well stated in the traditions and the community dimensions stressed.[42] Jean-Marc Ela, like Bujo, also develops a theology geared toward the community wellbeing in an African context.

---

39. Ibid., 22.
40. Ibid., 115–16.
41. Ibid., 29–32.
42. Ibid., 34.

Jean-Marc Ela: An African Appropriation of Liberation Theological Method

Jean-Marc Ela bases his theology on his experience among the people of Northern Cameroon. His theology is a response to a situation of oppression and injustice. He directs his attention to analyzing the situation of poverty and oppression and making suggestions on how to bring about a radical transformation. He states:

> My reflection on faith is rooted in the beginning of my experience in the north. A theologian must stay within earshot of what is happening within the community so that community life can become the subject of meditation and prayer. In the end, a theologian is perhaps simply a witness and a traveling companion, alert for signs of God and willing to get dirty in the precarious conditions of village life.[43]

Although Ela does not identify his theological method as based on the Latin American liberation theology, his theology is nonetheless similar to the liberation approach. African theology, according to Ela, should help establish the relevance of Christian teachings in an African worldview. It consists of the expression of the Christian faith through African languages and symbols. Ela states:

> If Christianity wants to reach Africans, to speak to their hearts, and to enter their consciousness and the space where their soul breathes, it must change. To do so, Christianity must do violence to itself and break the chains of Western rationality, which means almost nothing in the African civilization of the symbol. Without some form of epistemological break with the Scholastic universe, Christianity has little chance of reaching the African.[44]

Like Nyamiti and Bujo, Ela also argues that the "cult of the ancestors" in Africa is a basis for dialogue between Christianity and African traditions. According to Ela:

> An understanding of kinship also provides a vision of the world in which human beings are intended to transcend earthly limitations. The key moments in the cult of the ancestors maintain the communal ties that bridge the crevasse of death. In a society where everything is within a sacred cosmic order, the ancestors are

---

43. Ela, *My Faith as an African*, 10.
44. Ibid., 41.

remembered at the critical moments in the life of a person or the community... The profound meaning of the cult of the ancestors becomes clear when it is placed in the context of the African family, which is the foundation of its culture. Thanks to the kinship system, they remain linked to their families and continue to protect the living, caring for them and acting as their intermediaries, while receiving their respect, reverence, and solitude.[45]

In the *African Cry*, Ela takes the example of the Eucharistic celebration in an African context as depicting the alienation of the people. He holds that the Eucharistic celebration depicts the dependence of Africa on foreign thoughts and practices. "The Eucharist is real only in the transformation of a divided people into the oneness of Christ."[46] However, he is critical of the ritual of Eucharistic celebration, which he suggests needs to be acculturated. "The rite we follow has not been of our choosing; it bears the mark of a culture not ours; it has not developed in function of our personality or the genius of our people. And so the Eucharist on the life of the church has become the locus of our daily alienation."[47] The Eucharist celebrates the saving act of Jesus Christ. It should be celebrated in a way that promotes and transforms the life of the local community. Ela is critical of the un-inculturated celebration of the Eucharist, which he refers to as embodying a form of domination. He writes, "Thus the case of the Eucharist reveals the domination at the heart of the faith as lived in Africa, within a Christianity that refuses to become incarnate in our peoples."[48] Further, he criticizes the dependence syndrome when he maintains, "A dependent church among oppressed peoples—this is the global context in which the gospel must be reread today and in which the new tasks of Christianity in black Africa must be defined."[49]

Ela has clearly expressed his concern about African cultural alienation. He sees alienation as going back to the missionary movement of the modern times.[50] He cites slavery and colonialism as factors that have had a negative effect on Africa both culturally and socially. "The mis-

---

45. Ibid., 17. See also Bujo, *African Morality at the Age of Inculturation*, 75; and Nyamiti, *Christ as Our Ancestor*, 9–21.
46. Ela, *African Cry*, 1.
47. Ibid., 3–4.
48. Ibid., 5.
49. Ibid., 6.
50. Ibid., 10–11.

sions were aimed at youth, too; it was thanks to schools that Christianity spread through Africa. Adults resisted the incursions of a religion that overthrew the entire traditional social structure. The task of the missions was to attack the socio-cultural obstacles of the African world, showing the young the irrationality of the ancestral practices, the fatuity of the beliefs to which their parents were so attached."[51] Ela critiques the cultural imperialism that took place through the process of evangelization and colonization of Africa. He brings in the respect of cultural heritage as an important component of liberation because "Theology is a labor of deciphering the sense of revelation in the historical context in which we become aware of ourselves and our situation in the world."[52] He advocates for "an African reading of Exodus."[53]

Therefore, from the neglect of and even dismissal of African cultural heritage as incompatible with Christianity, Ela shows that the work of some early missionaries was not as effective as it should have been:

> The God of missionary preaching was a God so distant, so foreign to the history of the colonized peoples. Exploited and oppressed, they find it difficult to identify this with the God of Exodus, who becomes aware of the situation of oppression and servitude in which the people find themselves. The primary role of the Bible, and of the Old Testament in a special way, in African religious movements is to express the reaction and revolt of African Christians within the institutional churches in which the despised, humiliated human being lives a relationship to God under the rubric of absence.[54]

The relevance of Christianity in the African context of alienation, suffering, and oppression is to be seen in its contribution to the integral transformation of society and this way avoid what Ela has referred as "the strange God." This struggle between church missionary proclamation and the reality on the ground is referred by Ela as the tension in history between promise and fulfillment.[55] Unfortunately, if Christianity is viewed as justifying oppression and servitude, how can the people take refuge in the churches? Ela describes the confusion in many African

51. Ibid., 19.
52. Ibid., 28.
53. Ibid.
54. Ibid., 29.
55. Ibid., 35.

social and religious contexts as follows, "In short, rural Africa has recourse to religion in order to surmount the servitudes and the fear that weigh upon its daily life. Amidst uprootings and insecurity, the return to the old religious practices and ancestral beliefs attests to the permanence of a religious capital that changes in African society have not been entirely able to destroy."[56]

Consequently, Ela condemns the use of Christianization as an ideological tool for expanding European capitalism.[57] He argues that the use of Christianity as a tool for domination led to the founding of independent churches as a reaction. He advocates for the gospel of Jesus Christ as the tool for liberation and not a means of control and of curtailing people's freedom. He suggests, "We must rediscover the gospel as a decisive force in history's march to the fore. In a context in which dominant and dominated peoples are locked in confrontation, the task of the church consists in revealing to human beings the face of Jesus the Liberator in a faith practice and gospel rereading that will truly concretize the solidarity of the church with the poor and oppressed."[58] However, despite Ela's criticism, a word of caution on missionary movement is warranted: Putting missionaries as a group in the same category with colonial rulers in history is inaccurate and does not do justice to men and women who embraced harsh and deadly conditions to spread the Christian gospel and other charitable causes, such as schools and hospitals.

Besides being critical of colonialism and the missionary movement in Africa, Ela also notes that African post-colonial governments have oppressed their citizens, poor peasants, and unfortunately, this has been done through the help of foreign (European) nations and multi-national companies who have interests in natural resources and manpower in Africa. Referring to Frantz Fanon's *Wretched of the Earth* (trans. Constance Farrington [New York: Grove, 1968]), Ela argues that the transformation of life is only possible through peasant uprising or revolution.[59] However, this can lead to violence, and Ela does not delve into the availability of other peaceful alternatives, such as democratic participation of the people in shaping their lives.

56. Ibid., 41.
57. Ibid., 42.
58. Ibid., 53.
59. Ibid., 54–80.

In a critical way, Ela emerges in his work as a strong advocate for justice on behalf of the poor people of Cameroon. Toward this end, he argues that the African church has the right to be different and to have structures that are meaningful in an African social and historical context. He emphatically notes, "Hence the question of the identity of African Christians ought to be restored to the center of reflection on the relation between Africa and the gospel."[60] He gives as an example that Christians who are married according to the African customary marriage and not according to the sacrament of marriage as defined in the Church are considered to be living in sin.[61] The church should "break free of all of the colonial structures that weigh upon it in the African context."[62] For the church to be relevant in contemporary Africa, Ela suggests: "The church must find its ways of expressing its faith in a basic articulation between popular culture and the liberation of the popular masses, which have remained close to their mores and traditions."[63]

However, Ela has also critiqued the advocates who call for a return to the glorious past of Africa. He views the idea of adaptation or acculturation of Christian faith as empty if it looks only to the African past without paying attention to the present. He writes, "Free thought calls for the initiation of debate and for confrontation in all areas of public life. And so recourse is had to a theory that returns Africans to their past to keep them from facing the problems of the present. In actual fact, the search for an African identity is a search for a mythological past, which, for that matter, has never been well known except through the works of European ethnologists."[64] He views this as what constitutes alienation and oppression of Africans. Instead of dealing with the issues that contribute to their problems in society here and now, they are led to the "good old days" of their ancestors. Ela critically points out, "In being deprived of all opportunity to criticize the prevailing system, they are deprived of their genuine authenticity, left to wallow in ignorance of their alienation. They are sent off on a journey to a mythical past; otherwise they might take too close a look at their present, with its colonial exploitation at full tilt, albeit

---

60. Ibid., 113.
61. Ibid., 113–14.
62. Ibid., 118.
63. Ibid., 130.
64. Ibid., 126.

in disguised form."[65] An example of this would be the late Mobutu Sese Seko's initiative that made the people of Congo (formerly Zaire) to revert to their traditional names, not paying attention to how Mobutu himself was oppressing the same people. Ela states:

> The return to the past is a vast entertainment project, whose purpose is to distract the exploited masses from the struggles of the present. It is a manipulation of the past. It renounces a critical approach to tradition. African identity is not a heritage handed down. It is the deed of historical subjects, who transform themselves as they transform the world in which they live.[66]

Reading the work of Ela, one cannot avoid seeing the paradox of how culture and traditions can be oppressive and domineering and at the same time liberating. Cultures and traditions are empowering and therefore lead to liberation, but they can also be used as a tool for domination and exploitation. There is always a need for transformation or change at the individual and social level. For example, Ela argues that economic alienation is an evil to be fought. "In our world there is no autonomy in the area of culture without autonomy in the area of economy."[67] Hence, "We must believe in Jesus Christ, and put up a mighty resistance to all structures of oppression."[68]

Ela's two books cited in this section seem to be methodologically connected to one another. The two books should be read together. *My Faith as an African* seems to be a foundation for understanding *African Cry*, although *African Cry* was published earlier in English than *My Faith as an African*. *African Cry*, which was published in 1986, seems to advocate *praxis* in African Christianity, while *My Faith as an African*, published in 1988, seems to dwell on foundational issues. *African Cry* seems to advocate transformation of situations of poverty, oppression, and suffering. However, it does not show how either Christian communities or civil societies are to bring about positive social transformation. On the other hand, *My Faith as an African* seems to be "more tranquil" and deals with foundational issues in African Christian theology. In *My Faith as an African*, Ela is concerned with the issues that promote the meaningfulness

65. Ibid., 127.
66. Ibid., 129.
67. Ibid., 134.
68. Ibid., 138.

and relevance of Christian doctrines in Africa. For example, Ela notes: "The question then of an African symbolism to express the Christian message is the demand of a faith that is open to the concrete realities of people and their world."[69]

In conclusion, Ela overall connects an African theological foundation to the praxis of the Christian faith. The work of a theologian like Jean Marc Ela is of great contribution in Christian theology in Africa. The challenge to African Christianity is well laid out in his work. The task of applying and living faith without neglecting the social issues that affect human living is a perennial necessity. The work of the Tanzanian theologian, Laurenti Magesa, also fits into the development of African theology as seen in the works of Ela, Nyamiti, and Bujo.

Laurenti Magesa: The Ethics of Abundant Life in Africa

Laurenti Magesa has also pointed out that African theology is inseparable from African traditional religions. He presents African religion as entirely a lived religion and not a doctrinal one. A person is born into it and learns it from childhood throughout one's life and through normal socialization. Every word or act is understood in terms of good or bad (i.e., whether it is an attitude or behavior that enhances or diminishes life).[70] This is based on reflection on the experiences of the community and what is considered reasonable.

It is somehow similar to the natural moral law reasoning as developed by St. Thomas Aquinas where good is to be done and evil to be avoided. The religious reverence to the world and all that is in it is a moral requirement. For, according to Magesa, the world is a manifestation of God. The first and most important participation of the human person is in and through one's community.[71] The notable word here is Magesa's use of the word "participation," for it reflects Thomas Aquinas, who sees the natural law as a participation in the eternal law.[72] He acknowledges an order in the universe when he writes, ". . . to callously disturb created order by abusing it disrespectfully means nothing else, ultimately, than to

---

69. Ela, *My Faith as an African*, 51.
70. Magesa, *African Religion*, 60.
71. Ibid.
72. Aquinas, *Summa Theologiae*, I–II, q. 91, a. 2.

The Christological Foundation in African Inculturation Christian Theology

tamper dangerously with human life ... (and) ... if the world is disturbed, God, the spirits, and the ancestors ... are likewise unsettled."[73]

Magesa quotes Mbiti's statement, "I am because we are; and since we are, therefore I am,"[74] to show the guiding principle of African people's ethical behavior as based on the community. Consequently, he says that "religion is human-centered, even overtly utilitarian in the communal rather than the individualistic sense, and its officials are charged with the responsibility to see to it that this well-being endures."[75] This does not mean humanity is to treat the non-visible sphere or other creatures without respect but that they must realize the need to be in harmony with the universe, obeying the laws of the natural, moral, and mystical order, for if these are disturbed, people suffer the most.[76]

Magesa evidently acknowledges that the African peoples "have come to these conclusions through long experience, observation, and reflection."[77] In this interpretation of the natural world, he makes reference to the respect and sacredness that is associated with human life even in its conception, birth, and naming, and how it is a communal event.[78] Magesa also maintains that initiation rites are "divine services" that incorporate the moral code of the ethnic group and "symbolizes the unification of the whole tribal organization" and that the ". . . primary purpose of this instruction through wisdom is . . . to impress upon the initiates the intimate connection between human life and the rest of creation."[79] The proverbs, riddles, songs, dances, and other sources of ancestral wisdom are good sources of moral instruction. The young people are taught how to respect life and more especially concerning sexual morality.

From Magesa's perspective, African theology has to deal with issues that affect human living in society. He writes: "Theologically and in our Christian behaviour, our *Kairos* in Africa mandates that we discern our present socio-political and economic environment. This forms the infra- and super-structure of our understanding and following of Christ."[80] For

73. Magesa, *African Religion*, 61.
74. Ibid., 64.
75. Ibid., 69.
76. Ibid., 71–72.
77. Ibid., 74.
78. Ibid., 82–84.
79. Ibid., 96–97.
80. Magesa, "Christ the Liberator and Africa Today," 81.

Magesa, Christianity is not just the intellectual doctrines but also a way of life. He states:

> If we Christians have not been able to exhaust the demands of the Gospel of Jesus Christ in our comprehension here in Africa—much less fulfill them in action—there is then presented to us by that very fact a continual task to search ever more diligently, to try to understand ever more completely, to endeavor to live more perfectly our dedication to the very same Christ Jesus whom we profess. This we are called to do, following numerous factors or graces which deepen our vision of Him and His demands.[81]

Magesa also adopts the method of liberation theology. Like Ela, Magesa is concerned with the praxis of Christian faith in Africa. In a special way for Magesa, the Christ-event becomes the model for praxis in Africa. "The self-emptying of God in Jesus (cf. Phil. 2:6–8) is a matter of commitment and solidarity. By becoming human in Jesus, God's dedication to the exaltation of the human race and all creation became manifest."[82]

The developments in African theology are good signs of the process of inculturation. However, theology is never complete because new historical circumstances call for new ways of theologizing. Even as it is today, African theology has not yet fully solved the complicated questions of understanding the person of Jesus Christ and his teachings in an African historical context.

PART TWO

The Problem of Viewing Jesus as Ancestor

This section raises some questions on the African ancestor Christology. The understanding of Jesus as the ancestor is an attempt at inculturation of the Christian faith in African theology. However, the ancestor Christology is not without some difficulties, and it is with an awareness of the difficulties involved in inculturation Christology that I raise the concern of whether viewing Jesus Christ as the African ancestor provides a better way to understand the Christian gospel in Africa.

---

81. Ibid.
82. Ibid., 87.

The Christological Foundation in African Inculturation Christian Theology

The Christian mystery of the incarnation is that God became a human being in the person of Jesus of Nazareth. More precisely, Jesus Christ is believed to be both divine and human. Through the humanity of Christ, God is understood to have revealed himself to humankind in the world. The humanity of Christ provides the avenue to the knowledge of God for human beings. "But when the fullness of time had come, God sent his Son, born of a woman, born under the law, to ransom those under the law, so that we might receive adoption" (Gal 4:4–5). However, the incarnation of Christ remains a mystery attested to in the historical controversies and councils of the Church such as Nicea dealing with the heresy of Arianism, and Chalcedon dealing with the two natures (humanity and divinity) of the person of Jesus Christ. However, in Nicea and Chalcedon, the fathers resorted to the Greek philosophy to solve the problem of the two natures in Christ. Words such as *homoousios*, meaning Jesus Christ is of the same substance (or nature) with God the Father, are from Greek philosophy.[83] Nonetheless, the study of the person of Jesus Christ has to be based in the testimony of the sacred Scriptures and the faith tradition in the Christian history. Sacred Scripture is the "soul" of Christology while philosophy and other disciplines are aides at analyzing the Christian message on Jesus Christ.

The humanity and divinity of Christ constitutes the revelation of the mystery of God. I find ancestor-Christology as complicating more the mystery of the incarnation of Christ. African ancestor beliefs are mysteries in themselves. The main issue of concern seems to be that ancestor-Christology uses one mystery, namely the ancestors, to explain another mystery (the incarnation). However, one can respond that ancestor-Christology is a historically conscious method, since it uses African understanding of the spiritual world, the living dead, as they are called by John S. Mbiti. The ancestors are conceived of as members of a community who have passed on through death into the spirit life—hence, the traditional African belief that ancestors remain members of their respective communities (some sort of the communion of saints).

The understanding of the ancestor life is itself shrouded in mystery. What kind of life do the dead (ancestors) live? One can raise a number of issues with the use of ancestorship in reference to Jesus. Should African theology not be satisfied with the mystery of incarnation as it is, namely,

---

83. See O'Collins, *Christology*, 176–83.

in Jesus of Nazareth God became a human person? Is it logical to use one mystery to explain another mystery? Is an African understanding of a human person in community not a strong enough foundation for understanding the mystery of the incarnation?

The development of African theology is a noble task. However, the task of theology should always be to promote understanding of the Christian message. Theology is faith seeking understanding, and therefore it should not be used to complicate the basic teachings of the Christian faith. Nonetheless, the theological task of inquiry is also the task of African theology. Theology in Africa should be faith asking critical questions in an African perspective. In an African setting, theology has to concern itself with understanding God and humanity through African images. Inculturation of Christian teaching is a perennial necessity, especially in Africa. The challenge in African theology is to remain contemporary and historical at the same time, and thereby remain relevant to a people's everyday life.

Do we need to study the dead (ancestors) or the living people who have to confront the problems of daily living in order to develop an African Christology? The concern with the past should be aimed at dealing with issues at hand and in the future. In the book of Exodus, God is the God of the Hebrew people's fathers who has come to rescue them from their present misery (Exod 3:6–10). Realistically, it seems more helpful to focus on the living people rather than the dead. African theology should concern itself with what it means to be a living human person and this way contribute to the eradication of dehumanizing factors, such as those deriving from poverty (famine, disease, refugees). An African theology geared toward what Vatican Council II calls the humanizing aspect of culture[84] has the duty of promoting the physical and spiritual dimensions of human living.

Focusing on an African way of being a human person, African theology can lead in a radical way to the respect of human life. To promote the standard of living in society is part of the God-given mission to all human beings. Vatican Council II emphasized humanity's responsibility to make the world a better place to live. The Council fathers states:

> By the work of his hands and with the aid of technical means man tills the earth to bring forth fruit and to make it a dwelling place

---

84. Flannery, "Church in the Modern World" (*Gaudium et Spes*), no. 53.

> fit for all mankind; he also consciously plays his part in the life of social groups; in so doing he is realizing the design, which God revealed at the beginning of time, to subdue the earth and perfect the work of creation, and at the same time he is improving his own person; he is also observing the command of Christ to devote himself to the service of his fellow men.[85]

The Christian gospel is supposed to be the soul of transformation leading to the realization of human dignity created in the image and likeness of God (Gen 1:26–27). However, the preceding is a task that is always open to development and application in a historical context.

Changed Time and Inculturation in an African Setting

What are African traditions? This question leads to asking the opposite question: What is un-African? Usually, in many African countries, anything that is considered morally questionable or even any change is somehow seen as foreign and even to be as a result of western influence. The argument here is that African traditions consist of the various ways of daily living and deliberations that have come to be accepted by the people as authoritative norms guiding communal life. Traditions and customs consist of specific norms a group of people has decided as guidelines to their way of life. Tradition is formed by the people. For example, in Christianity there are issues in the contemporary world such as war and weapons of mass destruction, terrorism, reproductive technologies, etc., that the gospels in the New Testament do not provide a direct answer. However, Christians continually apply the teachings of Jesus to the new and changing situations they find themselves in. The Christian gospel becomes a guiding principle to Christians all over the world. Through reasonable dialogue, people come to agree or disagree on what is good or bad, what is morally right or morally wrong.

Received traditions are never in their final stage of development. The Church through the ages has continued to form new traditions. Old traditions become the launching pad for new ones. The same can be said of African traditions. New traditions in Africa are replacing older traditions. Some people who were pastoralists and led a nomadic lifestyle have settled as farmers or become urban dwellers. Their traditions from when they were pastoralists have evolved to new traditions now that they are farmers. African Christian theology is not to focus on traditions as fixed

85. Ibid., no. 57.

and unchanging beliefs and practices. True theology has a dynamism that reflects the people's changed attitudes and times.

A critical analysis of the relationship between theology and local traditions is always an on-going process. Good theology remains relevant in its social and historical context depending on how well it engages that context. African theology has to pay special attention to African traditions. Its task is to express Christian faith in a way that befits an African context. Traditions are a product of a people's reflection on their life and its interaction with the surrounding world. For traditions to be meaningful, they have to be reasonable. For African theology to be relevant and meaningful in an African setting, critical analyses of the received tradition are necessary. Some traditional customs in any society age and die a natural death. For example, female circumcision is extinct in some African ethnic groups that used to practice it.

Through a critical look on African traditions, now and in the past, African theology can be a forum of giving birth to new traditions that are both African and Christian at the same time. Self-determination of a people consists of constant change and development in thought and action. Unfortunately, African traditions have somehow been presented as stagnantly unchanging. What we call traditional customs and practices have themselves evolved through contact with people from different regions of Africa and outside Africa. But the most important point is an understanding that it is the people who are the source and the developers of traditions.

From the above, it is understandable that with time African traditions and cultures have been changing. Some cultural customs such, as polygamy, have been undergoing a slow natural death. Urban life and the contemporary form of education also have led to cultural transformation either for better or worse. Ela states: "Ethnologists are increasingly aware that it is unusual to find an African society whose activities are undisturbed by change. What will happen to the festival of the Bull tomorrow in northern Cameroon? Belief in the ancestors is also threatened by increasing urbanization."[86] The reality of cultural change is emphasized also in the work of Tom Mboya, the Kenyan trade unionist and politician who was assassinated in 1969. He referred to all the changes happening to

---

86. Ela, *My Faith as an African*, 24.

The Christological Foundation in African Inculturation Christian Theology

the newly independent African nations as the crisis of confidence. Mboya wrote:

> For us it is more difficult. To grasp at superficialities will not help. Is a man promoting African culture because he wears an ostrich feather or a beaded cap and sandals? Is it particularly African to wear fabrics which a designer in Hong Kong thinks suitable for this market; or to put a piece of animal skin over a Western suit or to wear some Muslim attire with your European clothes? Or, to put it the other way round, is an African not an African because his wife chooses some Western fashion, because he prefers modern plumbing or Western furniture in his home? What we need to do is to develop a culture based on the African traditions, yet not shunning international contacts and developments. We must not confuse poverty with culture for there is no point in clinging to practices and habits which arose merely from a lack of something better.[87]

Because culture is perennially changing in Africa as elsewhere, inculturation of the Christian gospel is also always a continuous process. An emphasis on ancestor Christology can lead to viewing the Christian gospel as out of touch with the majority of contemporary Africans. However, appealing to modern categories of thought in Africa can promote the understanding of the Christian gospel. This would incorporate the people's understanding of themselves and their concerns. Basically, theology should reflect life just as art imitates life.

Further, ancestor-Christology lays much emphasis on the cultural customs of the past without showing how the same has changed. It could be said to be an old mirror that makes one feel good by distorting the reality of who you are now (but sometimes images in the mirror are closer than they appear). I do not deny the importance of history in theological work, but it is my view that it is the human person in the present who interprets the past. It is from the present that one can look back to the past. The human person is the mirror that looks back to history to understand the present. But there is always the need to look at the present surroundings and what lies ahead, so as to be able to move forward. Cultures develop over time, resulting in to changes of beliefs and practices.

From the fore-going, an African theologian has to be careful not to seem disconnected from the people she/he serves through theological

---

87. Mboya, *The Challenge of Nationhood*, 17–18.

study. A well-informed African theologian is one able to articulate in a systematic way the experiences of his or her faith community. African theology, most of all, should be people-centered. Although theology is not a commodity, it should be people or user-friendly. In African theology there is need to avoid being prescriptive—the theologian studies, critically analyzes, interprets, and evaluates the experience of the people—that is, their faith and cultures or worldviews. The theologian's role is not to dictate what the people's belief, understandings, and practices should be. But he or she studies the life of the people.

Consequently, theology in Africa has to demonstrate the relevance of the Christian message in an African cultural setting. It is no news that Jesus was not born in Africa. Neither was he born in America, Europe, or Asia. He was born in Palestine (Middle East). Jesus is not an African ancestor by biological generation. However, his humanity and divinity make him transcend geographical borders and nationalities. Besides through faith in his divinity, one can say that the humanity of Christ puts him in relationship with all human beings on the face of the earth. The same can be said of all human beings, who all are related through a shared common human nature.

Besides saying who Jesus is in an African context, ancestor-Christology has not developed a method to show how other Christian doctrines, such as resurrection and ascension, are to be understood. For example, does the belief in the resurrection of Jesus Christ from the dead not apply uniquely to him? Is the risen Christ to be understood in the category of an African ancestor? Does the ancestor-Christology take analogy too far? How about the ancestors who in their lifetimes on earth led a sinful or criminal life? The intention here is not to discredit developments in contemporary African theology but to show the need for further development.

Human Experience as a Way to Understand the Significance of the Person of Jesus Christ in Africa

The ancestors have been presented as a way to understand the person of Jesus Christ in Africa. However, this is only true among some theologians, as seen in the previous section, and neither is it reflected in the practice of all Christian communities in various parts of Africa.[88] On his research on

---

88. See Magesa, *Anatomy of Inculturation*, 21–22.

The Christological Foundation in African Inculturation Christian Theology

inculturation in East Africa, Magesa states: "There was a mixed reaction from the respondents concerning belief in the ancestors and in mystical ancestral power."[89] What Elizabeth Isichei says of the Maasai is also notable:

> Where most African peoples had a cult of ancestral spirits, and interred the dead with care, the Maasai practised no burial at all, and corpses were abandoned to the hyenas. One might have expected their lack of concern for ancestors to predispose them to religious change, but, in fact, by the 1960s, Christianity had made virtually no impact at all, such as was their intense cultural patriotism and conservatism.[90]

To understand the person of Jesus Christ is the core foundation of any Christian community. This understanding is inseparable from a people's culture. The understanding of Christ as an African ancestor is as a result of the theology of inculturation. One may ask why in African Christology human experience and reasoning has not being emphasized much. Without reference to human history, experience, and reason, recourse to the ancestors for teachings would appear to be vague and distant—in the sense of being abstract and with no basis in contemporary reality. There is no concrete way of showing that the ancestors are active in the life of their progeny. Ancestor-Christology could also further an authoritarian style in theological study where the words and deeds of past ancestors are unquestionable and their misdeeds are incorporated in the community. Should reason not be an authority in evaluating what is relevant to a Christian community or in theological study?

Furthermore, there are as many ancestors as there are people in any African community. Whose ancestors take precedence over the others? Practical reasoning is a helpful way to approach theological issues. Jesus said, "You have heard that it was said . . . but I say unto." African theologians also have a responsibility to be conscious of the Christian community's capacity to understand and concretely apply the gospel to their daily living. It is the human person situated in particular circumstances who rationally considers an issue in light of the prevailing conditions. Human reasoning is a capacity in human beings to situate themselves in context and to respond to issues that face them. Through human living in society,

---

89. Ibid., 21.
90. Isichei, *A History of Christianity in Africa*, 260.

there is the possibility of realizing the relationship of human existence, the world, and God.

Besides ancestor theology, African experiences provide a sound basis for an African Christology. For example, African experiences of a contrast, such as unjust suffering, oppression, and general human alienation, are a foundation for showing the significance of Jesus Christ in an African context. "Experiences of suffering are experiences of a contrast."[91] Kasper holds, "The question of Christ and therefore the question of God as well is placed within the framework of the question of salvation."[92] African theology has a task to address African experiences of contrasts and discern the way to eliminate the social ills that dehumanize African people.

Conclusion

This chapter calls for a critical evaluation of culture and customs in the development of an African theology. Some of the emerging African theologies begin with an assumption that the knowledge of the human person, the ancestors, the community, and God are a given in African traditions and customs. However, any knowledge presupposes the people who bring it about through formulation of concepts and principles. It is not enough to say, "This is what our ancestors did and therefore I should do the same." There are questions that beg to be answered. How did the traditions of the ancestors come into being? What influenced an African community's worldview? Who were these people? In their lifetime, the ancestors themselves formulated their beliefs and moral norms through intelligent interaction with their world and human relationships. There is need for a dynamic and progressive way of developing an African theology.

The issue of method in African theology is one that requires a thorough consideration if any progress is to be made. This study does not claim to have solved issues in African theology; it only raises questions for further study. To be convincing, any theology should have a good methodological foundation, and this is what I have explored in this work.

The community setting in African theology is not to be taken as a way of avoiding deeper questions on the validity of the various cultural traditions and customs. People make culture through thoughts and practices. People respond to issues in their lives and thereby come up with a

---

91. Kasper, *The God of Jesus Christ*, 160–61.
92. Ibid., 158.

system of thought or a way of life. Cultures and customs are also a result of thought processes. African theology appeals in a special way to African cultures and traditions. Traditional religions of Africa are viewed as the foundation of the study of theology in an African context. However, cultures or traditions are dynamic in nature. People's lives change due to changing circumstances, and this change shapes their worldviews.

A suggestion is made here that besides sacred Scripture and traditions, African theology has to continually appeal to critical thought as a solid foundation and thereby promote the meaningfulness of Christian theology in Africa. The contextual nature of theology is only possible when subjected to reason. This, in a special way, shows the possibility of theological dialogue. The emphasis on the reasonableness of theological thought does not exclude the cultural aspect. African traditions and cultures need a critical analysis and evaluation to foster a theology that is contextual and at the same time reasonable. In African theology, the past history, cultural practices, and traditions of the ancestors are not to be emphasized to the detriment of present historical situations. To focus solely on the "good old days" and not deal with contemporary issues would be some sort of daydreaming. Hence, the study of theology is shaped by concrete reality as experienced in the lives of the people.

In a fundamental way, an African theology requires a good anthropological foundation. Anthropology here refers to an African understanding of what it is to be a human being. This also incorporates cultural practices in human living in society as well as the social-religious worldview. Of great importance to the study of theology in Africa is continued attention and recognition of culture and history. For example, the experiences of the nomadic Maasai of Kenya and Tanzania is different from the experiences of the farming Chaaga of Northern Tanzania or the urban Igbo in Nigeria. Finally, Africa needs many theologies that are attuned to various cultural and social diversities.

Bibliography

Aquinas, St. Thomas, *Summa Contra Gentiles and Summa Theologiae*. Translated and edited by Anton C. Pegis. *Introduction to St. Thomas Aquinas*. New York: Modern Library, 1946.

———. *Summa Theologiae*, Translated and commentary by R. J. Henle, S.J. Notre Dame: University of Notre Dame Press, 1993.

Augustine, "The Compatibility of Christianity and Politics." In *Political Writings*. Translation by Michael W. Tkacz and Douglas Kries, 202–12. Indianapolis: Hackett, 1994.

Barnett, Donald L. *Life Histories from the Revolution Kenya, Mau-Mau. The Hardcore: The Story of Karigo Muchai* (#1), 5–11. Richmond, BC, Canada: LSM Information Center, 1973.

———. *Life Histories from the Revolution, Mau-Mau: The Story of Ngugi Kabiro* (#2), 10–75. Richmond, BC, Canada: LSM Press, 1973.

Boff, Leonardo. *New Evangelization: Good News to the Poor*. Translated by Robert R. Barr. Maryknoll, New York: Orbis Books, 1991.

Boesak, Allan A. *Farewell to Innocence: A Social-Ethical Study on Black Theology and Black Power*. Maryknoll, NY: Orbis Books, 1977.

Bokenkotter, Thomas A. *A Concise History of the Catholic Church*. Garden City, NY: Doubleday & Co., 1977.

Borg, Marcus. *The God We Never Knew: Beyond Dogmatic Religion to a More Authentic Contemporary Faith*. San Francisco: HarperSanFrancisco, 1997.

Bujo, Bénézet. *African Christian Morality at the Age of Inculturation*. Nairobi: Paulines, 1990.

———. *African Theology in its Social Context*. New York: Orbis, 1992.

———. "A Christocentric Ethic for Black Africa." *Theology Digest* 30:2 (Summer, 1982) 143–46.

———. *Die Begründung des Sittlichen: Zur Frage des Eudämonismus bei Thomas von Aquin*. München: Ferdinand Schöningh, 1984.

———. *The Ethical Dimension of Community: The African Model and the Dialogue Between North and South*. Nairobi: Paulines, 1998.

Carr, Anne. *The Theological Method of Karl Rahner*. Missoula: Scholars, 1977.

Fiorenza, Francis Schüssler. "Introduction: Karl Rahner and the Kantian Problematic." In *Spirit in the World*. Edited by William Dych, xix–xlv. New York: Continuum, 1994.

Cone, James H. *Risks of Faith: The Emergence of a Black Theology of Liberation, 1968–1998*. Boston: Beacon Press, 1999.

Ela, Jean-Marc. *African Cry*. Maryknoll, NY: Orbis Books, 1986.

———. *My Faith as an African*. Maryknoll, NY: Orbis Books, 1988.

Flannery, Austin. *Vatican Council II: The Conciliar and Post Conciliar Documents*, Revised Edition. Dublin: Dominican, 1988.

Bibliography

Giblin, Sr. Marie. "Ujamaa Village Apostolate," In *Ujamaa and Christian Communities*, edited by Bishop C. Mwoleka and Fr. Joseph Healey, 43–50. Eldoret, Kenya: Gaba, 1976.

Gutiérrez, Gustavo. *A Theology of Liberation: History, Politics and Salvation*. Translated and edited by Sister Caridad Inda and John Eagleson. New York: Orbis, 1973.

Isichei, Elizabeth. *From Antiquity to the Present: A History of Christianity in Africa*. Grand Rapids, MI: Eerdmans, 1995.

Kameeta, Zephania. *Why, O Lord? Psalms and Sermons from Namibia*. Geneva: World Council of Churches, 1986.

Kang'ong'oi, Bertha. "Visit to Holy House of the Meru Elders." *Daily Nation* (June 20, 2005). Online: http://www.nationmedia.com.

Kasper, Walter. *The God of Jesus Christ*. Translated by Matthew J. O'Connel. New York: Crossroad, 1984.

Katjavivi, Peter. "The Role of the Church in the Struggle for Independence" In *Church and Liberation in Namibia*, 3–26. London: Pluto Press, 1989.

Kelly, Kevin. "Elections: Kenya an anchor for Africa." In *The East African*. No pages. Accessed on March 14, 2005. Online: http://www.nationmedia.com/east African.

Kimani, Peter. "Uganda's Children of the Night Sucked into an Orgy of Violence." In *Daily Nation*. Accessed on June 16, 2005. Online: www.nationmedia.com.

Lane, Dermot. *The Experience of God: An Invitation to Do Theology*. New York: Paulist, 1981.

Livingston, James C. *Modern Christian Thought*. Upper Saddle River, New Jersey: Prentice Hall, 1971.

Magesa, Laurenti. *African Religion: The Moral Traditions of Abundant Life*. Maryknoll, NY: Orbis Books, 1997.

———. *Anatomy of Inculturation: Transforming the Church in Africa*. Maryknoll, NY: Orbis Books, 2004.

———. "Christ the Liberator and Africa Today." In *Jesus in African Christianity: Experimentation and Diversity in African Christology*, edited by J. N. K. Mugambi and Laurenti Magesa, 79–92. Nairobi, Kenya: Initiatives Ltd., 1989.

Mazrui, Ali A. "Is African Development Plannable?" In *On Heroes and Uhuru-Worship: Essays on Independent Africa*, edited by Ali A. Mazrui, 137–45. London: Longmans, 1967.

Mbiti, John S. *African Religions and Philosophy*. Second Edition. Oxford: Heinemann, 1990.

Mboya, Tom. *The Challenge of Nationhood: A Collection of Speeches and Writings*. New York: Praeger, 1970.

Metz, Johann Baptist. *Faith in History and Society: Toward a Practical Fundamental Theology*. New York: Crossroad, 1980.

Mieth, Dietmar. "Solidarity and the Right to Work." In *Concilium. Unemployment and the Right to Work*, edited by Jacques Pohier et al., 58–65. Edinburgh: T. & T. Clark, December 1982.

Migliore, Daniel L. *Faith Seeking Understanding: An Introduction to Christian Theology*. Grand Rapids, MI: Eerdmans, 1991.

Miller Ed. L., and Stanley J. Grenz. *Fortress Introduction to Contemporary Theologies*. Minneapolis: Fortress, 1998.

Moltmann, Jürgen. *Creating a Just Future: The Politics of Peace and the Ethics of Creation in a Threatened World*. London: SCM Press, 1989.

Bibliography

———. *Following Jesus Christ in the World Today: Responsibility for the World and Christian Discipleship*. Occasional Papers No. 4. Elkhart, IN: Institute of Mennonite Studies, 1983.

———. *Theology of Hope: On the ground and the Implications of a Christian Eschatology*. Minneapolis: Fortress, 1993.

Mosala, Itumeleng J. "Race, Class, and Gender as Hermeneutical Factors." *SEMEIA: an experimental journal of biblical criticism*. 73 (1996) 43–57.

Mugambi, J. N. K., and Laurenti Magesa. "Introduction." In *Jesus in African Christianity: Experimentation and Diversity in African Christology*, edited by Mugambi, J. N. K. et al., x–xvi. Nairobi: Initiatives Ltd., 1989.

Muga, Wycliffe. "Just a Minute—Kenya's Colonial History Not Yet Told." In *Daily Nation Newspaper*. No Pages. Accessed on July 15, 2006. Online: nationmedia.com.

Mwoleka, Bishop Christopher. "Small Christian Communities and Human Promotion." In *Ujamaa and Christian Communities*, edited by Bishop Christopher Mwoleka et al., 18–33. Eldoret: Gaba Publications, 1976.

Nyamiti, Charles. "African Christologies Today." In *Faces of Jesus in Africa*, edited by Robert Schreiter, 3–23. New York: Orbis Books, 1991.

———. *African Tradition and the Christian God*. Eldoret: Gaba, 1978.

———. "Contemporary African Christologies: Assessment and Practical suggestions." In *Paths of African Theology*, edited by Rossino Gibellins, 62–77. Maryknoll, NY: Orbis Books, 1994.

———. *Christ as Our Ancestor, Christology from an African Perspective*. Gweru: Mambo Press, 1984.

———. "The Problem of Evil in African Traditional Cultures and Today's African Inculturation and Liberation Theologies." *African Christian Studies* 2 (March 1995) 39–75.

Nyerere, Julius K. "National Property." In *Freedom and Unity/Uhuru na Umoja: A Selection from Writings and Speeches 1952–65*, 53–58. London: Oxford University Press, 1967.

———. "The Courage of Reconciliation: The Dag Hammarskjöld Memorial Lecture." In *Freedom and Unity/Uhuru na Umoja: A Selection from Writings and Speeches 1952–65*, 266–85. London: Oxford University Press, 1967.

O'Brien, David J., and Thomas A. Shannon. *Catholic Social Thought Documentary Heritage*. New York: Orbis Books, 1992.

O'Collins, Gerald S.J. *Christology: A Biblical, Historical, and Systematic Study of Jesus*. New York: Oxford University Press, 1995.

Odhiambo Atieno, E.S., and John Lonsdale. *Mau Mau & Nationhood: Arms, Authority & Narration*. Eastern African Studies. Nairobi: EAEP, 2003.

Olupona, Jacob K. "African Religions and Global Issues of Population, Consumption, and Ecology." In *Visions of a New Earth: Religious Perspectives on Population, Consumption, and Ecology*, edited by Harold Coward et al., 175–99. Albany: State University of New York Press, 2000.

Rahner, Karl. *Foundations of Christian Faith*. New York: Crossroad, 1982.

———. "Reflections on Methodology in Theology." In *Theological Investigations*, Vol. XI. Translated by David Bourke, 68–114. London: Darton, Longman & Todd, 1974.

———. "Theological Anthropology." In *Theological Investigations*, Vol. VI. Translated by Karl-H and Boniface Kruger, 178–96. Baltimore: Helicon, 1969.

———. "Theology and Anthropology." In *Theological Investigations*, Vol. IX. Translated by Graham Harrison, 28–45. London: Darton, Longman & Todd, 1972.

Bibliography

Ratzinger, Joseph Cardinal (now Pope Benedict XVI), "Instruction on Certain Aspects of the 'Theology of Liberation.'" Rome: Vatican City, August 6, 1984. No Pages. Accessed June 1, 2008. Online: www.vatican.va/roman_curia/congregations/cfaith/documents.

Schreiter, Robert J. *Constructing Local Theologies*. New York: Orbis, 1985.

The Canon Law Society of Great Britain and Ireland. *The Code of Canon Law*. London: Collins Liturgical Publications, 1983.

The Roman Missal: The Sacramentary. English Translation prepared by the International Commission on English in the Liturgy. New York: Catholic Book Publishing Co., 1974.

Tillich, Paul. *The Courage To Be*. New Haven: Yale University Press, 2000.

Waliggo, John M. "African Christology in a Situation of Suffering." In *Jesus in African Christianity*. Edited by J. N. K. Mugambi and Laurenti Magesa, 93–111. Nairobi, Kenya: Intiatives Ltd., 1989.

Wamwere, Koigi. "Parliament in Dire Need of Urgent Reforms." *Daily Nation* (June 29, 2005). Accessed July 20, 2005. Online: http://www.nationmedia.com.

Weger, Karl-Heinz. *Karl Rahner: An Introduction to his Theology*. New York: The Seabury, 1980.

World Almanac (Editor), *World Almanac and Book of Facts* 2000. Mahwah, NJ: Primedia Reference Incorporate, 1999.

OTHER ONLINE SOURCES:

http://www.geocities.com/orthopapism/lumko.html.

"An African Model for Bible Study (or the Lumko method, after the Institute which promotes it)," in the website: http://home.earthlink.net/~haywoodm/biblestudymethods.html. See also the Ignatian Method of Bible Study in the same website.

http://www.adherents.com/adhloc/wh-2.html.

The Catholic University of Eastern Africa. Accessed August 5, 2007. Online: www.cuea.edu.

The National Council of Churches of Kenya. Accessed September 8, 2006. Accessed January 18, 2008. Online: http://www.ncck.org/homepage.